CONSUMER PRODUCT SAFETY STANDARDS AND CONFORMITY ASSESSMENT

Issues in a Global Marketplace

ORGANISATION FOR ECONOMIC CO-OPERATION AND DEVELOPMENT

ORGANISATION FOR ECONOMIC CO-OPERATION AND DEVELOPMENT

Pursuant to Article 1 of the Convention signed in Paris on 14th December 1960, and which came into force on 30th September 1961, the Organisation for Economic Co-operation and Development (OECD) shall promote policies designed:

- to achieve the highest sustainable economic growth and employment and a rising standard of living in Member countries, while maintaining financial stability, and thus to contribute to the development of the world economy;
- to contribute to sound economic expansion in Member as well as non-member countries in the process of economic development; and
- to contribute to the expansion of world trade on a multilateral, non-discriminatory basis in accordance with international obligations.

The original Member countries of the OECD are Austria, Belgium, Canada, Denmark, France, Germany, Greece, Iceland, Ireland, Italy, Luxembourg, the Netherlands, Norway, Portugal, Spain, Sweden, Switzerland, Turkey, the United Kingdom and the United States. The following countries became Members subsequently through accession at the dates indicated hereafter: Japan (28th April 1964), Finland (28th January 1969), Australia (7th June 1971), New Zealand (29th May 1973), Mexico (18th May 1994), the Czech Republic (21st December 1995) and Hungary (7th May 1996). The Commission of the European Communities takes part in the work of the OECD (Article 13 of the OECD Convention).

Publié en français sous le titre :
NORMES DE SÉCURITÉ POUR LE CONSOMMATEUR ET ÉVALUATION DE CONFORMITÉ DES PRODUITS
Enjeux sur un marché mondial

FOREWORD

Issues involving consumer product safety standards and conformity assessment, such as testing, certification and accreditation, have assumed greater importance with the regionalisation and globalisation of economies. In light of these developments, the OECD Committee on Consumer Policy has conducted a comprehensive investigation to gather information on the nature and extent of issues and problems in this area. This initiative follows upon previous work in this area published in a report entitled "Consumers, Product Safety Standards and International Trade" (OECD, Paris 1991).

The primary objective of this project is to encourage the highest standards of consumer protection. Within this framework, this publication attempts to define consumer interest, and to challenge the assumption that there is a fundamental contradiction between consumer safety and reduction of barriers to trade. The Committee on Consumer Policy hopes that this publication will provide a basis for discussion, as well as a starting point for further exploration of issues within this area.

The Executive Summary and Suggestions for Action are based on:

-- data collected in a survey conducted by the Committee on standards and conformity assessment for four categories of consumer products: toys, home appliances (based on the example of microwave ovens), outdoor power equipment (lawn mowers) and personal protective equipment (bicycle helmets). The results of the survey are described in Part II of this publication;

-- substantial contributions by representatives of government, industry, standards and safety bodies, and consumer organisations for a conference on the effect of consumer product safety standards and conformity assessment on international trade, held under the auspices of the OECD in Paris in December, 1995. These contributions are included in Part II of this publication;

-- extensive experience of the European Community in this area, which is described in Annex 2; and

-- invaluable input by the OECD Steering Committee on Standards and Consumer Safety, comprised of representatives from government, industry and consumer organisations, whose expertise, initiative and spirited discussion provided the analytical framework for this project. The OECD Committee on Consumer Policy would like to thank the governments of

3

Finland, Japan, the Netherlands, Norway, Sweden and the United States for their generous financial contributions to this project.

This report is part of an ongoing OECD project on "Consumers in the Global Marketplace." The goal of this project is to identify consumer concerns in a rapidly changing environment, and promote, together with OECD governments, industry and consumer groups, the highest levels of consumer safety and protection. It is published on the responsibility of the Secretary-General of the OECD.

Table of Contents

Part I

EXECUTIVE SUMMARY

1. Executive summary

A number of encouraging developments have taken place since the publication of the last OECD report in this area in 1991. Probably the most important of these has been the entry into force of the World Trade Organisation Agreement on Technical Barriers to Trade (TBT) and Annex 3 Code of Good Practice for the preparation, adoption and application of standards which contain many of the principles established in the previous OECD report on promotion of the use of international standards. But despite these considerable developments, standards, regulatory requirements and conformity assessment continue to be perceived by business and regulators alike as non-tariff barriers to trade.

International standards have still to find widespread acceptance in some major markets. In addition, because of concerns that standards may not satisfy national or regional safety requirements, the functional equivalence of differing standards is seldom mutually accepted. Thus, industries have to manufacture products to a multitude of different standards and technical specifications resulting in higher costs which are ultimately passed on to the consumer. Consumer choice can be reduced as some manufacturers are effectively prevented from entering markets. The way standards are drafted can also exacerbate this problem. Overly prescriptive standards can stifle technical development and innovation to the ultimate disadvantage of the consumer.

A lack of international acceptance of the results of testing and conformity assessment procedures hampers international trade. Repetition of product testing often provides no greater guarantee of safety, but instead increases costs and delays, and can even prevent manufacturers from introducing products into the marketplace. Voluntary certification schemes, which in practice can sometimes be required by the demands of the marketplace, may also present problems. This can occur, for example, if the organisations granting certification refuse to accept the results of foreign testing bodies, or prevent the use of quality marks to which they hold the intellectual property rights.

In considering future steps in these areas, it is important to remember that in principle the primary objectives of product safety standardisation measures -- whether mandatory requirements imposed by public authorities or market-driven voluntary requirements -- is to ensure that consumers in a given market receive the level of quality and safety that they expect, and that at the same time manufacturers are able to sell into that market with a clear understanding of what is required of them. Proposed measures should neither preclude alternative or innovative ways of achieving equivalent or better levels of quality, nor impose unnecessary additional costs which will ultimately be borne by consumers.

Both consumers and manufacturers then benefit. Consumers can expect greater choice, reduced costs and an atmosphere which encourages technical innovation and diversity while guaranteeing their basic right to safety. Manufacturers can market products across the globe without unnecessary repetition of testing and certification procedures.

Based on research described in this publication, a number of conclusions can be drawn from the following report. These include:

A. *Use of standards*

In the case of mandatory and regulatory requirements, there appears to be a consensus that policy objectives are best achieved by regulations which specify broadly expressed safety requirements. The use of voluntary standards then offers a recognised means of demonstrating conformity with those requirements. This is the approach pioneered in the European Union with the Low Voltage Directive and adopted in the "New Approach" in 1985.

The use and acceptance of international standards is expanding and market forces will help promote this, but further expansion is necessary. Where possible national standards should be harmonised with existing standards promulgated by the International Organisation for Standardisation (ISO) and the International Electrotechnical Commission (IEC) when they offer acceptable levels of protection. Results of this research show that international harmonisation does not have to mean lowered safety or quality standards, which is the often expressed fear of consumers.

Standards should where possible be prepared on the basis of performance requirements which specify acceptable parameters within which a product must function under normal conditions of use, rather than in terms of design or descriptive characteristics. This will ensure that standards do not stifle continued product innovation. Standards having equal effect should be recognised by the parties involved and not be subject to discrimination.

In this area, this report concludes that:

-- the use of standards in support of generally expressed regulations allows manufacturers maximum flexibility and helps avoid technical barriers to trade;

-- continued growth of international standards should be based on performance requirements, to ensure that standards do not stifle continued product innovation;

-- the standards drafting process can be improved in terms of speed, efficiency and relevance to consumer concerns and market conditions.

B. *Mutual recognition of conformity assessment procedures*

The existence of harmonised standards and technical regulations will not on its own necessarily guarantee free movement of goods onto different foreign markets. To ensure this, existing standards should also be recognised as equivalent. If there are differing requirements for the testing and certification of products, either for mandatory or market-driven reasons, these can impede trade and cause manufacturers to incur unnecessary extra costs, which are ultimately passed on to the consumer.

Conformity assessment, whether by first, second or third parties, is essential to show proof of conformity to standards. In cases where third-party assessment is required, mutual recognition of testing and certification can greatly reduce needless repetition of conformity assessment procedures and duplication of certification. Mutual recognition agreements (MRAs) between governments, between conformity assessment bodies, and between accreditation bodies are an important step towards meeting consumer and market demands, and can provide a model and frame of reference for agreements covering mandatory requirements.

The use of mandatory third-party certification in particular increases costs to the producer. In response, the European Union, for example, has promoted expanded use of the manufacturers' self-declaration of conformity in its directives adopted under the New Approach. This liberalisation operates best when supported by systems of market surveillance. Third-party testing is still imposed, however, with products where this is necessary to ensure the required levels of consumer safety.

In this area, this report concludes that:

--   multiple testing and certification greatly add to cost, and can delay or prevent products from being introduced into the market place. For mutual recognition to succeed, it is necessary to ensure the competence of testing and certifying organisations and to monitor them;

--   to ease regulatory burdens, greater use of the manufacturers' self-declaration of conformity should be made where this is consistent with ensuring a high level of consumer safety. It is important to monitor manufacturers' observation of standards through appropriate surveillance of the market;

--   mutual recognition of conformity assessment procedures may be the most efficient method of reducing product costs and increasing consumer choice while ensuring uniformly high standards of product safety;

--   competition authorities may wish to examine the granting of voluntary marks under national and international rules governing the restraint of trade and competition;

--   barriers to trade can result when organisations granting voluntary marks do not accept the results of equivalent foreign testing.

C. *Transparency*

Greater transparency is necessary in specifying the requirements products must satisfy before they can be introduced into the market. Transparency will be greatly enhanced to the extent that internationally recognised standards and technical regulations, together with common criteria for the functioning of conformity assessment bodies and accreditation bodies, are adopted.

The standards drafting process must also be transparent, and requires the active participation of industry, consumers, national administrations, insurers, etc. This is particularly relevant for voluntary standards and conformity assessment procedures that have been developed by the market itself. Such procedures should not be used for anti-competitive purposes, and must not discriminate against foreign producers.

Support must be given to those co-ordination initiatives on various levels, including the governmental and private sectors, which contribute to the transparency of decision-making procedures. These initiatives include notification requirements under article 2.92 of the TBT Code, the International Collaborative Effort on Injury Statistics, the World Health Organisation Working Group on Injury Surveillance, the International Working Group on Product Safety Research established by European Consumer Safety Association, and the Codex Alimentarius working party examining the standardisation of enforcement practices. There is also a need for co-ordination among these different initiatives.

The main participants in the marketplace, in particular industry, need to understand the underlying infrastructure in the standardisation and conformity assessment area to ensure that all parties capitalise on measures adopted to ease regulatory burdens.

In this area, this report concludes that:

-- there is a lack of understanding among industry and other market participants of the provisions of existing trade instruments on standardisation and conformity assessment;

-- greater transparency is required at all levels in standards development, particularly to guarantee that standards are not used for anti-competitive purposes;

-- all relevant parties, including consumer representatives, need to be more closely involved in standards development in order to ensure the acceptance of standardisation efforts in the marketplace. Information about standards development should be presented in a timely fashion and in a manner easily accessible to consumer representatives;

-- de-regulation by public authorities should not be replaced by de facto private sector "regulation" which restrains competition;

-- additional research in specific product areas is needed in view of the growing importance of these issues.

2. Suggestions for action

The OECD Committee on Consumer Policy deals with major international policy issues arising in the areas of consumer protection, information, representation and redress, and the inter-relation between consumer policy issues and general economic policy. It has no intention of participating in the technical process of product standardisation or defining the details of conformity assessments regimes. Its role in the efforts towards international harmonisation of safety standards for consumer goods and acceptance of conformity assessment procedures is necessarily determined by its capacity to deal simultaneously with the consumer protection and international trade implications of product-related safety measures. On the basis of the present study, the Committee believes that action to address these issues should include the following measures:

A. *At the level of Member countries*

Member countries should:

-- encourage the establishment of mechanisms for the mutual recognition of conformity assessments made in different countries, thereby reducing the expense associated with multiple testing and certification of products;

-- exchange information on national and regional product safety standards to facilitate transparency, and assist consumers and industry in assessing the safety requirements within an individual marketplace;

-- elaborate national standards within existing international standards as outlined in the WTO Technical Barriers to Trade Agreement and Code of Good Practice for the Preparation, Adoption and Application of Standards. Standards should embrace a high level of consumer protection, and where possible, be performance-based so as not to stifle innovation. Where standards are called up in technical regulations, standards of equivalent effect should also be accepted;

-- monitor the competence of testing organisations and manufacturers to ensure strict adherence to safety standards;

-- support enforcement of relevant legislation in the interest of both consumer safety and fair competition in the market;

-- recognise that unwillingness on the part of a standardisation or conformity assessment body to accept results from a foreign body may reflect a competition problem;

-- ensure full implementation of the requirement in the WTO Technical Barriers to Trade Agreement and Code of Good Practice. When adopting mandatory technical regulations, voluntary standards and conformity assessment procedures for the protection of consumers, choose the least trade-restrictive measures possible while taking into account the risks that non-fulfilment of that objective would create;

-- solicit the active participation of national administrations, producers, distributors and retailers, and consumer groups in the creation and acceptance of standards. At the national level consumer input should continue to be encouraged and supported at all stages of the regulatory and standardisation process, especially in the identification of priorities, the definition of basic safety requirements and the enforcement of existing obligations;

-- promote a greater understanding of current market infrastructures in relation to standards and conformity assessment, especially where these have been affected by the WTO Technical Barriers to Trade Agreement and Code of Good Practice;

-- co-ordinate existing initiatives, for example in the fields of the exchange of accident data, product safety research and product safety enforcement.

B. At the level of international and inter-governmental organisations

International and inter-governmental organisations should:

-- elaborate international standards according to the WTO Technical Barriers to Trade and Code of Good Practice for the Preparation, Adoption and Application of Standards. Standards should embrace a high level of consumer protection, and where possible be performance-based so as not to stifle innovation. Where standards are called up in technical regulations, standards of equivalent effect should also be accepted;

-- solicit the active participation of national administrations, producers, distributors and retailers, and consumers groups in the creation and acceptance of standards. Consumer input at the international level should continue to be encouraged and supported at all stages of the regulatory and standardisation process, especially in the identification of priorities, the definition of basic safety requirements and the enforcement of existing obligations;

-- improve the international standardisation process to increase the speed and efficiency with which standards are drafted and approved. The market relevance of standards programs should be reviewed, and when necessary, changes should be adopted;

-- develop agreements for the mutual recognition of test results and certification and for the accreditation of testing houses and bodies carrying out conformity assessment procedures

C. At the level of the OECD

The Committee on Consumer Policy should:

-- ensure that the views and conclusions contained in this report which are relevant to the issue of regulatory reform be reflected in other OECD work, including the multi-disciplinary programme on regulatory reform now underway;

-- explore issues relating to the regionalisation of standardisation and conformity assessment systems, and their consequences for consumer safety and trade. These may include proliferation of marks, confusion by consumers and industry about the significance of marks, and intellectual property issues related to marks, competition, consumer safety and trade;

--   facilitate dialogue with interested non-OECD countries on the conclusions of this report;

--   analyse the effect of increased information and consumer education as a cost-effective enhancement or substitute for regulation;

--   evaluate the effects of marketing practices regulations such as comparative advertising on consumer access to information in cases where products substantially exceed prescribed safety standards;

--   explore the relationship between insurance issuers and marking and certification practices;

--   discuss additional measures to maintain and increase consumer confidence in product safety.

Part II

ISSUES IN PRODUCT SAFETY STANDARDISATION
AND CONFORMITY ASSESSMENT

1. Background

Issues involving product standards and conformity assessment, such as testing, certification and accreditation, have assumed greater importance with the regionalisation and globalisation of economies. Traditionally, standardisation and its related concepts have been addressed by policymakers from two points of view. First, consumer organisations and regulators have concentrated on issues of product safety and consumer protection. Second, standardisation has been considered by international trade authorities in the general context of its effect on trade. These issues have been further complicated by the emergence of standardisation and conformity assessment as a substantial international business and the development of marks as commercial products.

In light of these developments, the OECD Committee on Consumer Policy has conducted a comprehensive investigation to gather first-hand information from business and government on the nature and extent of issues and problems in this area. Product safety officials, manufacturers, trade associations, standardisation bodies and conformity assessment organisations have been surveyed on the effects of product safety standards and related conformity assessment requirements in international trade.

The study focused on standards and conformity assessment for four categories of consumer products: toys, home appliances (based on the example of microwave ovens), outdoor power equipment (lawn mowers) and personal protective equipment (bicycle helmets). Ninety-five manufacturers of these products in 14 countries completed extensive questionnaires. An additional set of questionnaires were completed by trade associations, safety officials, and standards and conformity assessment bodies. An analysis of the responses received from product safety agencies is included in Part 2(A), and from manufacturers and trade associations in Part 2(B) of this section. The responses from manufacturers, trade associations, standardisation bodies and conformity assessment organisations were collated, and tables containing survey data are attached in Annex 1. The preliminary results of this survey were used as a basis for discussions held at the OECD Conference on "Consumer Product Safety Standards and Conformity Assessment: Their Effect on International Trade" in Paris on 7-8 December 1995. The final survey results, together with the speakers remarks found in Part III form the basis for the Suggestions for Action included in the Executive Summary of this publication.

The survey emphasises that one of the major stumbling blocks to discussing product safety standardisation and conformity assessment requirements is technical terminology. The terms used herein attempt to follow usage as defined by the International Organisation for Standardisation (ISO). An alphabetical list of acronyms used herein is included in Annex 3.

A. *Prior work by the Committee*

This initiative follows upon previous work in this area published in a report entitled "Consumers, Product Safety Standards and International Trade" (OECD, Paris 1991). In that report, the Committee found that "concern with product specifications acting as trade barriers is also amply documented by various contributions to the 1984 OECD Symposium on Consumer Policy and International Trade and the periodic reviews within the OECD Trade Committee of recent trade policy developments in Member countries. Pushed to the extreme, certain administrative entry procedures linked to compliance with national standards certification or testing procedures may serve to shelter national markets and cap the quantity of imports, sometimes even more effectively than quantitative restrictions."

The 1991 report also identified major trends and developments having a significant effect on standardisation and conformity assessment systems which provided the foundation for many of the issues addressed in the current document. These include:

Regionalisation:

-- "the creation of the internal European market is the most prominent among a number of examples of the strong impact of regionalisation in the development of standards. While the development of international standards through the ISO and the International Electrotechnical Commission (IEC) remains the ultimate objective of harmonisation, future developments in the area of standardisation will be strongly marked by the activities of the European standardisation bodies Comité européen de normalisation (CEN) and the Comité européen de normalisation électricité (CENELEC). The existence of a dominating political objective will affect the nature and the speed of harmonisation of national standards at the regional level. Whether and to what extent this will be detrimental to international harmonisation will largely depend on the relationship between regional and international standardisation" (p. 11).

Use of voluntary safety standards:

-- "in the past, product safety was considered a basic governmental responsibility which had to be exercised through mandatory safety regulations. Experience with product safety policy has shown that the quantity of regulatory work associated with mandatory regulations often exceeds the capacity of product safety authorities. Authorities now tend to leave the development of detailed safety specifications to non-governmental standardisation bodies or to the business sector concerned. This shifting of responsibilities to private standardisation has been accompanied in most countries by the introduction of a comprehensive product safety policy which generally includes some monitoring of the market, general product safety laws and powers to impose product bans and recalls.[1] Legal authority of this kind is the precondition for reliance on voluntary safety standards" (p. 12).

Mutual recognition of safety standards:

--   "the fact that technical specifications concerning the safety of consumer goods are not
identical does not necessarily imply that the products involved actually present different safety
levels. Divergence in definitions, specifications, test methods, etc. often result from
historically established preferences and manufacturing processes which do not always affect
the actual safety characteristics of a product. Complete consistency of safety standards may be
unnecessary from the standpoint of consumer protection, as long as basic safety expectations
are satisfied. Mutual recognition of safety standards, and as its logical consequence, [mutual
recognition] of testing and certification, can be welcomed by consumers as long as there is
agreement on these expectations.[2] This principle has been incorporated in the [European
Union's] "New Approach" (discussed in greater detail in Annex 2 on Standardisation and
Conformity Assessment in the European Community). Another solution to increase flexibility
would be to allow for partial harmonisation: where there is agreement on most features of a
standard, alternative but equivalent solutions can be included for remaining areas of
controversy" (p. 12).

The 1991 report concluded with a number of suggestions for action, all aimed at reducing the
potential for safety standards and conformity assessment requirements to become barriers to trade. In
particular, it recommended that mutual recognition of safety standards and conformity assessment
procedures be encouraged: "Relevant intergovernmental and non-governmental organisations should
increase their co-operation in the area of product safety with a view to defining criteria for mutual
recognition of standards, certification procedures and test methods" (p. 13).

Since issuance of the 1991 report, the Committee has noticed the growing importance of
standardisation and conformity assessment issues with respect to efforts at liberalisation of trade. One of
the most problematic issues associated with such efforts is how to maintain consumer confidence in the
safety of products available on domestic markets while allowing foreign products greater access to those
markets. International trade agreements such as the WTO Technical Barriers to Trade Agreement
(TBT), and regional agreements such as APEC, NAFTA and the European Union have each initiated
changes which affect the operation of standardisation and conformity assessment systems in different
ways.

B.   Identifying consumer and industry concerns on issues of product safety and trade

The placement of what used to be primarily consumer product safety issues in the larger context of
trade has made it easier to appreciate the convergence of the consumer and exporter interest in this
matter. While confidence in the safety of products available on the market is an essential consumer
concern, it is also in the consumer interest to ensure that the means of achieving that level of confidence
does not negate the benefits of open markets: greater choice and price competition among products.
Likewise, exporters of consumer products seeking access to foreign markets also have a strong interest
in promoting consumer confidence in the safety of their products.

Addressing consumer safety concerns about products available in open markets requires taking into
account the extent and dynamics of the global marketplace. The most obvious characteristic of the

global marketplace is the sheer quantity and variety of products available to the consumer, and the pace at which new products enter the market. It is important, therefore, to examine the impact of standardisation and conformity assessment requirements to ascertain the extent to which they delay the introduction of new products or even exclude them from various markets.

It is also important to consider the effect of changes in technology and commercial practices, including new methods of manufacturing and management of product safety, which call into question many of the assumptions that formed traditional product safety standardisation practices and procedures. Management of product safety problems must be adapted to the fast-paced developments in the global marketplace. Manufacturing processes have in many cases been thoroughly internationalised, and modern retail marketing practices and internal distribution often involve shipping merchandise across borders to meet consumer demand. The efficiencies of many of these developments can be limited by current conformity assessment requirements such as those which result in unnecessary re-testing of merchandise.

Adapting product safety standardisation and conformity assessment requirements to the global marketplace requires consideration of factors including the nature of the product, the user, the risk and the market. In the global marketplace, the role of general product safety laws, product liability, and insurance must be assessed for their effect on the behaviour of consumers and manufacturers and the resulting impact on safety. Consumer confidence in the efficacy of the standardisation and conformity assessment process can be enhanced by the efficient use of the many mechanisms currently available to address these issues. This may require a redefinition of these mechanisms within the context of a global marketplace to determine how they can best meet the needs of consumers and manufacturers.

Duplicative conformity assessment procedures or different national or regional standards that are costly or add little to product safety are not in the interest of consumers or exporters. Besides offering no additional consumer protection, these systems are burdensome and add delays and costs which must ultimately be passed on to the consumer.

An important focus of this effort is directed to the practical effects of product safety standards and conformity assessment on the functioning of the market. The experience of manufacturers of consumer products illustrates the problems involved in manufacturing and marketing products to specific safety standards and conformity assessment requirements. This input assesses the effect that such requirements have on product costs and export decisions, and provides data which suggest that the existing system of standards may have differing impacts on small, medium and large manufacturers, thereby exercising a direct competitive effect.

In the area of conformity assessment, the appropriate role and cost-effectiveness of third-party certification requirements is examined. Here, survey results suggest that in certain cases requirements by national and regional authorities may be so burdensome that they restrict international competition among testing and certifying bodies.

2. The OECD Survey

A. Methodology

The survey examines the actual experience of those most closely affected by safety standards and conformity assessment requirements to determine the extent to which they affect trade. The experiences of safety agencies, manufacturers, exporters, consumer organisations, trade associations and standardisation, accreditation and certification bodies has been sought on this question, as well as on the significance of recent developments in standardisation and conformity assessment systems. The issues explored are far ranging and include such questions as: the impact of producing consumer products to different product safety standards on small, medium and large manufacturers; the effects of product safety standards and conformity assessment requirements on product exports; the need for multiple accreditation for testing and certifying bodies; the cost and effects of industry involvement in the standards development process; and ways to improve standards and conformity assessment requirements, making them more cost-effective while ensuring product safety.

The first part of the survey involved a questionnaire designed to gather information from Member government product safety agencies about safety standards and conformity assessment requirements in their countries as they apply to the four consumer product areas.[3] The questionnaire sought information concerning particular safety standards (including the provisions of standards, date of adoption, institutions involved, equivalent international standards and enforcement provisions), conformity assessment requirements (including the type of certification, proof of conformity, enforcement provisions, institutions involved, requirements for accreditation and the conditions for acceptance of conformity assessment results), and existing or proposed agreements that would facilitate the acceptance of conformity assessment results.

The second part of the survey was distributed to manufacturers, trade associations, and standards organisations and conformity assessment bodies. Three separate questionnaires were developed by the Committee Secretariat and distributed by Member country Delegates to relevant manufacturers and organisations. The questionnaires were designed to obtain information to document the practical effects of safety standards and conformity assessment requirements on issues such as the propensity of small, medium or large manufacturers to export, to become involved in the standards development process, and to avoid or seek certain markets because of difficulties relating to standards.

B. Product safety agency surveys

(i) Safety standards

The organisational structure of standardisation systems in Member countries ranges from rather centralised systems involving very few institutions, such as in Turkey, to de-centralised systems involving many institutions, such as in Australia and the United States.[4]

Toys

Of the products surveyed and responses received, toys are the most intensely regulated in OECD Member countries. Every respondent country has safety standards for toys and many of those national standards are equivalent to international or quasi-international standards.[5] Toy standards appear to have been the subject of significant activity in recent years and all the respondent countries have reviewed or revised toy standards within the past five years.[6] Inconsistent responses from Delegates concerning toy standards indicated that the definitions of "mandatory" and "voluntary" are not entirely clear, especially as concerns CEN and CENELEC standards.[7] Toys sold in the European Union are subject to the mandatory EC Toy Directive and to voluntary CEN/CENELEC standards. In order to ensure that standards exist, the European Commission is able to ask CEN/CENELEC to give priority to the development of certain areas. Work is currently under way on an ISO toy standard. Toy standards in OECD Member countries are both performance and design standards.[8]

Microwave ovens

The level of equivalency to international standards applicable to microwave ovens is higher than for the other product categories surveyed.[9] Nearly all the responses indicated that national or regional standards applicable to microwave ovens are based on IEC standards. Standards applicable to microwave ovens in the European Union are found in the Low Voltage Directive (LVD)[10] and in standards developed by CENELEC. The CENELEC standards are equivalent to IEC standards. Conformance to the LVD is mandatory, while conformance to the CENELEC standards is voluntary.

Lawn mowers

Delegates responded to the survey with respect to both electric and petrol-driven lawn mowers. In the European Community, electric lawn mowers under the "New Approach"[11] are subject to the Low Voltage Directive (LVD) 73/23/EEC and both electric and petrol-driven lawn mowers are subject to the Machine Directive 89/392/EEC. Under the "Old Approach", a directive concerning sound emission applies. Technical standards for electric lawn mowers are currently being developed by CENELEC based on design and performance. They will be voluntary. Petrol-driven lawn mowers in the European Union are subject to the Machine Directive 89/392/EEC and to the Noise Emissions Directive 84/538/EEC (as amended by 87/252/EEC; 88/180/EEC; and 88/181/EEC).[12] The CEN standard (pr EN 836) on garden machinery, which corresponds to the international standard ISO-5395:1990 will be published in 1996, and will specify conformance with the Machine Directive.[13] The CEN standard will be voluntary and equivalent to the ISO standard. Lawn mowers in other OECD Member countries are subject to both mandatory and voluntary standards.[14]

Bicycle helmets

Bicycle helmet standardisation is currently being developed at a more specific level. Many countries have standards for personal protective equipment, but not for bicycle helmets in particular.[15] International standards for bicycle helmets do not exist.[16] Personal protective equipment (such as bicycle helmets) sold in the European Union is subject to the European Directive on Personal Protection Equipment (PPE) 89/686/EEC which sets forth essential safety requirements.[17] According to the directive, personal protective equipment is presumed to be in compliance with the directive if it conforms to CEN standards. CEN standards on personal protective equipment are under development and have not yet been promulgated. When completed, the CEN bicycle helmet standards will be voluntary performance standards.

Sanctions for non-conformance to standards

In general, all respondent countries have provisions to penalise companies that sell products that do not conform to mandatory regulations.[18] Officials of Member States in the European Union have a number of enforcement options to prevent the marketing of a product which fails to conform to European directives, including product warnings, recalls, fines and prison. Enforcement authorities may also have the options provided by general product safety laws, although the operation of general product safety laws in Europe and the United States call into question the "voluntary" nature of some standards. In the United States, Federal toy regulations are enforced with civil and criminal provisions. Manufacturers of products which do not conform to a voluntary standard may be subject to greater liability if the product causes harm.[19] In certain cases, such a defect may authorise the government to remove it from the market or take other measures. The United States does not have any penalties for selling a microwave oven which does not conform to voluntary standards, except in the State of Maryland. Conformance to Underwriters Laboratory (UL) standards, however, is strongly supported by the industry trade association and is very common. The Consumer Product Safety Commission (CPSC) has the authority to respond to the selling of microwave ovens that contain a defect which creates a substantial risk of injury. The full range of penalties is available in the case of non-complying lawn mowers.[20] In the European Union, the applicable requirements for conformance to standards on personal protective equipment are contained in the PPE Directive. The PPE Directive does not, however, include provisions that apply specifically to bicycle helmets. Consequently, current good practice and state of the art in the industry determine whether or not safety helmets comply with the PPE Directive. Selling bicycle helmets which fail to comply with the directive is a criminal offence and penalties include fines and confiscation of the goods.[21]

(ii) Conformity assessment requirements

Manufacturer's self-declaration of conformance is allowed in most of the respondent countries in their product areas.[22] In the European Union, manufacturer's self-declaration of conformance is permissible for toys if they conform with harmonised European standards. If the toy does not conform to the CEN standards, then third-party, EC-type examination is required. In the case of manufacturer's self-declaration of conformance, the manufacturer must be able to document that the product conforms to the standard. Beginning in 1997, in the European Union, microwave ovens and electric lawn mowers will require manufacturer's self-declaration of conformance to prove conformance with the LVD. Conformance of both electric and petrol-driven lawn mowers to the Machine Directive is done through manufacturer's self-declaration of conformance. The Machine Directive requires that a technical file be available for inspection.[23] The file must be able to document how the essential health and safety requirements have been met and must list any European or national standards used. Suppliers of petrol-driven and electric lawn mowers must produce an EC-type testing certificate showing conformance with the Noise Emission Directive. This requirement will also be extended to electric lawn mowers in 1997. Only notified bodies are competent to conduct EC-type testing for conformance to the Noise Emission Directive, but this is required only for machines falling under Annex 4, a small minority of lawn mowers.[24] Where the PPE is in effect for bicycle helmets, third-party testing is required. Pursuant to Article 6 of the PPE Directive, the party that first places a bicycle helmet on the market must be able to furnish a declaration of conformity, technical documentation and an EC-type examination certificate issued by an authorised body. The conformity assessment system for bicycle helmet standards in the European Union is no different from the system for lawn mower, toy or microwave oven standards except that testing by a notified body is required. In order to be designated a notified body, the testing and certification organisation must be able to meet the general requirements set out in the PPE Directive.[25]

In the European Union, mandatory conformity assessment is conducted by notified bodies that are generally accredited or notified by national accrediting bodies.[26] In the case of toys, the notified bodies must conform to EC Toy Directive 88/378.[27] In the European Union, in the framework of a New Approach directive, all conformity assessment bodies must be notified to the Commission, and they can be accredited (with reference to standard EN 45.011) by an accreditation body. These accreditation bodies are generally private law organisations, but their creation is supervised by the public authorities in each country. These bodies have organised themselves in the framework of the European Association for the Accreditation of Laboratories (EAL). The European Commission favours accreditation, but it is never mandatory. Mutual recognition of certificates from various testing bodies is currently a subject of negotiations between the European Union and third countries. In most cases in the European Union, third-party testing and certification is not required but is optional.[28]

In the European Union many, but not all, countries require that testing and certification organisations conform with the EN-45000 series of standards, which set out the criteria to be met by accreditation, certification, testing and inspection bodies, and only results from other EU notified bodies are accepted.[29] For products conforming to CEN/CENELEC standards, certain European countries accept test results from non-notified bodies.[30] For example, the Netherlands accepts test results from non-EU bodies conforming to certain EN-45000 standards, and test results from bodies which have entered into agreements with the Dutch Council for Certification are also accepted. Other OECD countries have differing conformity assessment systems.[31]

Denmark, Finland, the Netherlands, Portugal, Sweden, and Switzerland accept conformity assessment results from organisations that are members of the CB certification system of the IECEE and the CCA certification system of CENELEC. Finland also accepts testing and certification results from those participating in the Nordic Certification System. The European Co-operation for Accreditation of Laboratories (EAL) and the European Accreditation for Certification (EAC) have entered into agreements with Australia and New Zealand to accept each other's testing and certification results. Japan is part of the IECEE-CB system and the conditions required by MITI for acceptance of foreign testing and certification are based on that system.

The CE marking has been available for each of the four product categories since 1992/3 in order for them to be sold in the European Union. The CE marking on toys is a claim of conformity to the EC Toy Directive. The CE marking on microwave ovens is a claim of conformity to the LVD and Electromagnetic Compatibility (EMC) Directives. For both electric and petrol-driven lawn mowers sold in the European Union, the CE marking is a claim of conformity to the Machine Directive and for electric lawn mowers only a claim of conformity with the LVD and EMC Directives. Bicycle helmets sold in the European Union bearing the CE marking claim conformity with the PPE Directive.[32]

In the European Union, specific information regarding noise levels must appear on lawn mowers. In Germany, the Geprüfte Sicherheit mark (GS) is also available on a voluntary basis for each of the product categories. In Japan, toys must bear the ST mark, and in Turkey, the TS mark. In Japan, bicycle helmets bearing the SG mark show conformance to the voluntary standards. Japan requires microwave ovens and lawn mowers to bear a mark which signifies conformance with national standards. Toys, microwave ovens, lawn mowers and bicycle helmets sold on the Mexican market must bear the Norma Official Mexicana (NOM) mark and registration number or a mark of a private certification body, signifying conformance with official Mexican standards. All microwave ovens marketed in Portugal must bear the mark Portuguese Quality Institute (IPQ). Mexico, Japan and Turkey require third-party certification, signifying conformance with national mandatory standards. There are no legal requirements for testing and certification of toys in the United States. It is the responsibility of the manufacturer and retailer to ensure that a toy that does not conform to US toy regulations, or otherwise violates the Consumer Product Safety Act, is not placed on the market. There is no requirement for a certification mark on microwave ovens sold in the United States, although third-party certification organisations require that their mark appear on products that they have certified. In the United States, walk-behind lawn mowers must be labelled with specific production information as well as a general statement concerning conformity to the CPSC standards. The proposed mandatory bicycle helmet standard in the United States requires a conformance label.

There is not always a clear distinction in the European Union between non-conformance to the essential requirements affecting the product, and non-conformance with the conformity assessment requirements. The sanctions that enforcement agencies are authorised to seek when conformity assessment requirements are not followed include product warnings, recalls, fines and prison, although penalties for non-compliance with essential safety requirements will be much more stringent than those for non-adherence to conformity assessment requirements.[33]

With respect to the ISO 9000 quality management standards, none of the Member country responses indicated that toy manufacturers were required to be registered. Some countries do, however, strongly encourage conformance to ISO standards.[34]

C. Manufacturer and trade association surveys

Responses were submitted from 95 manufacturers in 14 OECD Member countries, including Australia, Denmark, Finland, France, Germany, Greece, Italy, Japan, Mexico, the Netherlands, Portugal, Sweden, the United Kingdom and the United States, and from trade associations in France, Japan, Mexico, Sweden, the United Kingdom and the United States (see Tables 1 and 2).

The largest number of responses came from toy manufacturers (see Table 3). Thirteen trade associations submitted responses (see Table 4). Manufacturers responding included toy manufacturers from Australia, Denmark, Finland, France, Germany, Greece, Italy, Japan, Mexico, Netherlands, Portugal, Sweden, the United Kingdom and the United States (see Table 5), lawn mower manufacturers from Denmark, France, Germany, Japan, Mexico, Sweden, the United Kingdom and the United States (see Table 6), microwave oven manufacturers from Germany, Japan and the United States (see Table 7), and bicycle helmet manufacturers from France, Germany, Mexico, Sweden and the United States (see Table 8).

Seventy-four per cent of responding manufacturers were small- and medium-sized manufacturers, defined as enterprises with total annual sales under US$ 100 million (see Table 9). Most small manufacturers were from Europe, while the largest respondents were from North America and Japan (see Table 10). The responses from trade associations indicated that most of their members are small- and medium-sized enterprises (see Table 11). In total, trade associations who responded represented 1089 individual firms.

Responding companies have experience manufacturing their products in Europe, North America, the Asia-Pacific region, and in Brazil, China and Russia. Twenty-four of the 95 responding companies manufacture in the United Kingdom, 22 in the United States, 17 in Germany, 12 in Japan and Mexico, nine in Italy, seven in France, and five each in Denmark and Sweden. In non-OECD countries, 25 manufacture in China and seven in Brazil. Responding trade associations had a similar geographical mix (see Tables 12 and 13).

There is broader representation in terms of where the respondents sell their products. The majority of respondents sell in almost every European country, while 70 or more of the 95 sell in France, Germany and the United Kingdom. More than half of all respondents sell in Canada and the United States, and almost 50 per cent sell in Australia, Japan and New Zealand. Many respondents are actively selling in developing markets, particularly Brazil and Russia (see Tables 14 and 15).

(i) Safety standards

When asked about safety standards applicable in their most important markets, respondents cited standards in the European Union, Germany, Japan, the United Kingdom and the United States. EN-71 was mentioned as the applicable toy safety standard for the European Union, Germany and the United Kingdom, and the majority of respondents view EN-71 as mandatory. Respondents also cited ASTM F963 and HD 271 for toys, and the CE mark and EN 836 for lawn mowers as applicable safety standards. Respondents showed disagreement on whether standards were mandatory or voluntary because even when they are legally voluntary, some manufacturers view standards as mandatory to preserve the reputation of the company and the product (see Tables 16 and 17).[35]

When asked why they would manufacture products that conformed to voluntary standards, respondents agreed that conformance to voluntary standards was important primarily to protect the company's reputation, for consumer safety, and to reduce the risk of legal liability. The least important factor cited in the decision to conform to voluntary standards is demand by end consumers (see Tables 18 and 19).

Manufacturers and trade associations were asked about the additional costs of manufacturing products to applicable safety standards in markets where they already sell their products, and in markets where they would like to sell. In addition, they were asked about the effects that applicable safety standards had on their ability to get new products onto the market quickly.

Concerning markets where they currently sell, 65 per cent of manufacturers agreed that manufacturing products to the relevant safety standards significantly increases the cost of the product.

Responses from trade associations supported this (see Tables 20 and 21). Thirty-eight per cent agreed that manufacturing products to the applicable safety standards reduces their ability to get new products to market quickly (see Tables 22 and 23).

Concerning markets where they would like to sell, 45 per cent of manufacturers that expressed an opinion were in agreement that manufacturing to the applicable standard would significantly increase costs. Manufacturers had stronger views with respect to North America, where 67 per cent of respondents expressing an opinion believe that manufacturing products to the applicable safety standards in North America would significantly increase costs (see Tables 24 and 25). Thirty-five per cent of manufacturers agreed that manufacturing products to applicable safety standards would significantly reduce their ability to get new products to market quickly in new markets. Trade associations were neutral as to whether manufacturing to a standard significantly reduced their ability to get products onto new markets (see Tables 26 and 27).

When asked for their views on possible changes to applicable standards to improve their safety or cost-effectiveness, many manufacturers suggested a harmonised international standard (based on, for example ISO standards, EU standards or US standards) in markets where they already sell and in markets where they would like to sell their product. A number of respondents suggested using a hazard-based approach in designing standards, using injury evidence as a basis for safety requirements and cost-benefit analysis for all non-injury evidential hazards.[36]

(ii) Development of safety standards

More than two-thirds of respondents indicated that they had participated in the development of one or more safety standards. A wide variety of standards in all four product categories were cited. They also indicated extraordinary variations in the cost of this participation, ranging from several thousand to over US$ one million.[37]

Respondents generally indicated that participation in standards development was a priority. They particularly cited a belief that their participation in the development of particular safety standards would have a positive effect on the resulting standard, as well as a concern that if they did not participate their views would not be heard (see Tables 28 and 29).

When describing why they chose not to participate in the development of a particular standard, a number of manufacturers indicated that high costs were a factor. More troubling were responses indicating a lack of awareness that the standard was under development or, worse, that the respondent was not permitted to participate in the process.[38] Many times, non-participation was due simply to the belief that the company could live with the standard that was likely to come out of the process (see Tables 30 and 31.)

(iii) Proving conformity to safety requirements

In response to the question concerning the most important markets where products are already being sold and the most common types of conformity assessment procedures required for those markets, the most frequently identified markets were the European Union, France, Germany, the United Kingdom and the United States. In each of these countries, manufacturer's self-declaration of conformance is accepted [39] (see Tables 32 and 33).

In those cases where the conformity assessment procedures were not required by law, respondents were asked to identify the reasons for voluntarily choosing a particular conformity assessment procedure. Manufacturers agreed that the most important factors are reduction of official barriers to sale in a given market, safety risks, the company's reputation and the quality of the product, while the least important factor is consumer demand. These results mirror the responses for product safety standards (see Tables 34 and 35).

Respondents were asked to identify the certification marks that appear on their products and then to identify what they believe consumers understand when they see the mark. The five most frequently mentioned marks were the CE mark, EN-71, the GS mark, and the TÜV and VDE marks. With respect to the CE mark, most manufacturers believe that consumers erroneously understand the mark to indicate that the product conforms to all government safety standards, that the product is safe and that product meets high quality standards. But at the same time, 32 per cent of manufacturers believe that consumers generally do not have any idea what the CE mark signifies [40] (see Tables 36 and 37).

Respondents were asked to identify which countries require registration of manufacturing facilities to the ISO 9000 or a similar series of standards in order to sell their products. [41] The responses did not clearly indicate a requirement for manufacturers' facilities to be registered to the ISO 9000 or similar series of standards in OECD Member countries (see Tables 38 and 39). In some cases, distributors and importers demand ISO 9000 certification. In the area of testing and certification, respondents were asked about the resources involved in meeting the conformity assessment requirements in their most important markets. They were asked to identify their most important market and describe how the product is tested and certified and to estimate the time and costs involved. Manufacturers mentioned most frequently the European Union, France, Germany, the United Kingdom and the United States as countries where their product is both sold and tested and/or certified, although testing and certification most often occurs in the country where the product is manufactured. The testing and certification process in the European Union and in Germany takes between one week and six months, depending on the precise nature of the product, at a cost of between US$ 200 and US$ 50 000. In the United States, manufacturers estimate between ten days and six months, at a cost of between US$ 200 and US$ 75 000. The costs of testing and certification may reach as high as US$ 150 000 in the United Kingdom. [42]

Respondents were then asked to indicate the impact of conformity assessment requirements for particular products on their costs and ability to introduce new products onto the market in markets where they currently sell. Sixty-six per cent of responding manufacturers agreed that testing and certification procedures significantly increase costs (see Tables 40 and 41). This is approximately the same number that agreed that applicable safety standards significantly increase costs. Forty-five per cent also believe that such procedures significantly reduce their ability to introduce new products to markets (see Tables 42 and 43). There were no significant differences in attitudes across the major markets.

Substantially fewer respondents answered the same question as it applied to markets they would like to enter. Of this group, 52 per cent of manufacturers agreed that current testing and certification procedures would significantly increase costs in these markets (see Tables 44 and 45). Thirty-seven per cent agreed that those procedures would significantly reduce their ability to get new products to market quickly (see Tables 46 and 47).

Respondents were asked to suggest possible improvements to conformity assessment procedures to increase their cost-effectiveness. Suggestions included one international standard in preference to harmonised conformity assessment requirements, mutual recognition of conformity assessment results world-wide to eliminate costly re-testing of products, and increased manufacturer's self-declaration of conformance to standards. Some microwave oven respondents specifically mentioned the VDE license in Germany and EMC testing, and criticised the high costs. Lawn mower respondents in particular expressed the need to enforce EU directives for competition reasons and the need for a mark to indicate conformance with the CEN standards. Comments from North American lawn mower manufacturers indicated a desire to have North American testing and certification results accepted in Europe. North American manufacturers also noted a difficulty with the notified body system, and indicated that they believe that a manufacturer's self-declaration of conformance to the Noise Emissions Directive should be permitted in Europe. One bicycle helmet respondent suggested that, with respect to Australia and Canada, "batch" testing requirements be changed to allow the manufacturer to perform them. Trade associations identified the importance of mutual recognition, the existence of one international standard and the harmonisation of network conditions (e.g. voltage, frequency etc.).

(iv) International agreements

The final section of the questionnaire explored the impact of international agreements and how they affected safety standardisation or conformity assessment procedures from the perspective of manufacturers and trade associations. Respondents were asked to identify aspects of international agreements that they believed had the greatest impact on safety standards and conformity assessment requirements and provide their assessment about the success of such agreements. The final question asked respondents to suggest improvements to product safety standardisation and conformity assessment procedures.

North American toy manufacturers in particular identified the Vienna Agreement which allows CEN standards to become ISO standards without the opportunity for non-Europeans to participate in the CEN process. They suggested that the Vienna Agreement be repealed. North American lawn mower manufacturers criticised the EU system. They drew attention to the problem of re-testing and called for a more open process in the European Union with the acceptance of non-EU test results and standards that are based on scientific and injury data. Microwave oven respondents identified several agreements including the CB and the UL/Canadian Standards Association (CSA) agreement. The CB system was cited for making it possible for manufacturers to test only once and have those test results accepted world-wide. The UL/CSA mutual recognition agreement was cited for making it possible for microwave ovens to be sold in either the United States or Canada with one certificate. One bicycle helmet manufacturer identified the adoption of a single helmet standard in the European Union as the most significant development from its point of view.

The majority of responding manufacturers agreed that there is a need to harmonise safety standards and a need to make it possible for product testing and certification results to be accepted world-wide.

Trade associations highlighted the need for mutual recognition. In an ideal situation, manufacturers would only have to contend with one safety standard, one test procedure and one approval mark throughout the world.

D. Standards and conformity assessment institutions

Responses were received from 43 standards and conformity assessment institutions in the following OECD countries: Australia, Austria, Canada, Denmark, Finland, Germany, Greece, Japan, Mexico, Sweden, the United Kingdom and the United States.

Respondents included standards writing organisations, and conformity assessment institutions who were active in testing and certifying products as well as registering manufacturers quality schemes. A smaller number of respondents were also involved in accreditation of product testing and certification organisations.   Three organisations was involved with accreditation of quality systems.   Two organisations dealt with the accreditation of standards development organisations. The spread of the respondents' activities extended beyond the OECD area into Brazil, China, India and Russia (see Table 48).

Seventy per cent of respondents were private organisations, of which 46 per cent were non-profit organisations. Only 12 per cent of the respondents described themselves as government agencies with seven per cent and five per cent describing themselves respectively as government funded but independent or a mix between government and private organisations.   International and regional organisations made up five per cent of the respondents (see Table 49).

(i) Product safety standards

Most responses came from organisations with involvement in toys (14), followed by bicycle helmets (11), microwave ovens (nine) and lawn mowers (seven) (see Table 50). Seventy-two per cent of the respondents came from Europe, 16 per cent from North America, and the remaining 12 per cent from the Asia-Pacific region (see Table 51).

A number of international regional and national standards were identified for the products covered by the survey. The most important international and regional standards and for toys were the European regional standard EN71,[43] for ovens the international standard IEC335-2-25,[44] and for bicycle helmets the draft European standard prEN1078.[45] For lawnmowers both a draft European standard (prEN836) and an international standard (ISO-5395) were identified.[46]

Respondents were asked about their level of involvement in the development of product standards. Existing industry, national, regional and international standards played a significant role in the development of new standards, and specific examples were given of the consideration of these standards.[47] Where standards had been wholly adopted a number of different reasons were given[48] (see Table 52).

Respondents were also asked to rate the importance of the role that different factors played in the development of product safety standards.   The participation of consumers, large manufacturers, government and large trade associations were all cited as factors that played an important role. Serious consideration was generally given to international standards in the development of national standards. The cost of conformity was not necessarily a major consideration (see Table 53).

The participation of foreign entities was generally welcomed, with some organisations having formalised rules governing this.[49] Others, such as ASTM in the USA, always welcome foreign organisations with no conditions.

Respondents were asked to comment on descriptive statements concerning particular product standards. In general respondents felt that the standards reflected the state of the art in the particular technology, but that there was not necessarily significant differences between different safety standards applicable to a particular product (see Table 54).

Regarding specific injury reduction associated with the identified product standards, several respondents gave examples where specific risks were addressed in the standards, and evidence of the effect of the action taken could be demonstrated through accident data collected since the introduction of the standard.[50] The opinion was voiced that it was generally accepted that standards did reduce injuries significantly.

When asked to identify changes that could be made to the identified product safety standards, a number of respondents cited specific examples.[51] The general need to review standards regularly in the light of current research and development was highlighted.

Respondents were questioned on their attitudes towards reducing differences among standards for particular products. Lack of interest, differences in present standards, rapid technological development in the market place, the time involved in developing a international standard, and the cost involved were not considered to be major obstacles to harmonisation (see Table 55).

Regarding the process of standards development, consumer participation was accorded high importance by respondents. Also important were the development of international standards, and providing general notice, an opportunity to comment during the development stage, participation by small- and medium-sized enterprises, and participation by foreign manufacturers and trade associations. Thorough risk analysis was generally considered to improve product safety standards (see Table 56).

(ii) International agreements

Respondents were asked to identify international agreements that have had an impact on their organisation's involvement with product safety standards. Respondents were then asked to identify the most significant parts of these agreements, and whether they had a positive or negative impact on the development of product safety standards. Finally respondents were asked whether they felt there was any need to develop new international agreements to reduce the differences between regional and national product safety standards.

Respondents particularly acknowledged the important role that the WTO-TBT Agreement and other regional free trade agreements had played in generally increasing the prominence of standards and highlighting the issues associated with standards and conformity assessment. Article 2.2 of the WTO-TBT agreement requires WTO-TBT members not to erect unnecessary technical barriers to trade. This is considered to be a great benefit to the development of product safety standards because it clearly states the signatory's obligations. It was felt that this resulted in a shift in strategy towards harmonisation of standards, particularly with international standards.

In Europe, the New Approach, which is extended under the EEA agreement to EFTA member states, greatly influences the standardisation process. Mandates are issued by the European Commission to the European standards organisations. There is then an obligation on member states' national standards bodies to implement the ratified European standards and remove any conflicting national standards. There are in addition co-operation agreements between European and international standards organisations, for example the Vienna agreement between CEN and ISO to allow for the transfer of work from the European to the international level to encourage harmonisation at the international level. For an elaboration of this area see Annex 2.

In the Asia-Pacific region the APEC agreement has given an impetus to align requirements among the different states. Between Australia and New Zealand there is a treaty agreement for closer economic relations (ANZCERTA) under which both countries agreed to remove non-tariff barriers. Within Australia itself there is a mutual recognition agreement between the commonwealth states and territories which has given impetus to harmonise standards.

The majority of respondents identified the need for greater international harmonisation. It did not appear from respondent's replies that this necessarily required new international agreements. Instead, respondents identified the need for a greater commitment to on-going international standardisation work while recognising the need to improve the speed and efficiency of the processes.[52]

(iii) Proving conformity to product safety standard

Respondents were asked to cite specific countries where testing results from their organisation were not accepted and asked to identify potential reasons for this. Respondents were able to identify a number of specific cases where product testing carried out by their organisation would not be accepted in third countries. For example, bike helmets tested in Sweden were not accepted in the United States. Microwave ovens tested in Mexico were not accepted in the United States and vice versa. Ovens tested in Denmark and the United Kingdom were also not accepted in the United States. Ovens tested in Australia were not accepted in Japan. It was claimed that this was for legal reasons and due to the demands of end purchasers, distributors and retailers. Toys tested in the United Kingdom and lawnmowers tested in Denmark were also not accepted in the United States. The majority of respondents to this question believed that it was impossible in some countries for any foreign testing facilities to be accredited (see Table 57).

Similar information was requested with regard to the certification activities of the respondents' organisations and specific cases were identified. For example, toys certified in Denmark and Finland and were not accepted in the United States and bike helmets certified in Sweden were not accepted in the United States. Mowers and ovens certified in Denmark were also not accepted in the United States for legal reasons and because of the demands of end purchasers, retailers and distributors. Responses suggest that obstacles to certification may include requirements by distributors and importers, and local regulations. The cost of the accreditation process did not appear to be a factor (see Table 58).

Respondents were asked to identify the cost of accreditation in relation to their testing and certification activities and responses varied from $86 to $20 000[53]. Significant costs were identified through the need for re-testing. Multiple accreditation and certifications, which were often necessary, increased cost while not appreciably improving safety. There was some agreement that accredited certification programmes should include consumer notification and recall provisions. Changes suggested by respondents to testing or certification procedures or practices to improve their cost-effectiveness or reliability included increased co-operation between those who drew up the standards and those who apply them[54] (see Table 59).

(iv) International agreements relating to testing and certification

Respondents were asked to identify those international agreements developed within the past ten years which had had an impact on their organisation's testing or certification practices and procedures. At the global level, a number of respondents identified the CB scheme of IECEE, under which testing results were accepted internationally. Registration to ISO 9001, 9002 and 9003 was also identified.

In North America it was suggested that NAFTA provides a framework to establish mutual recognition agreements reducing the use of standardisation and certification as trade barriers. Specifically between the United States and Canada, A2LA and SCC MRA were cited.

In Europe there are a number of voluntary agreement schemes. These include the long established CENELEC Certification Agreement (CCA) which regulates the application of national voluntary marks denoting compliance with standards. There are also other such schemes operating at a European level in different sectors such as the CECC for electronic components and the LUM scheme for lighting fixtures. This last group is falls under the framework of the European Organisation for Testing and Certification (EOCT). There are also European agreements between national accreditation bodies (EAL, EAC, and multilateral recognition agreements).

When discussing the international agreements, respondents were also asked to identify the most significant parts of the agreements they cited. A number of respondents stated that they believed that existing international agreements did contribute positively to the reduction of trade barriers.[55]

Finally, respondents were asked if there was a need to develop new international agreements. Proposals made by respondents included an agreement on accreditation between the European Union and the United States and an international agreement for the acceptance of accredited lab results, a first step to harmonising accreditation procedures to guarantee the same level of competence among certifying organisms. Further development in mutual recognition agreements between regional accreditation co-operation organisations was also proposed, with a possible first phase bi-lateral agreements between EAC-EAL with third countries. Other proposals included harmonised standards, the creation of one common safety mark, harmonised certification requirements and restrictions on national or private marks.

Obstacles to progress that respondents cited included mistrust, differences in manufacturing processes, and government politics (red tape). It was also felt that it would be difficult to reach agreement on an MRA applicable to lawn mowers as the standard was not yet harmonised.

E. Conclusions to be drawn from survey results

The responses from safety agencies, manufacturers and trade associations reveal a strong interest in many of the trade issues related to product standardisation and conformity assessment. The survey results also disclose frequent confusion, misunderstandings and differences in characterisation of the basic elements of standardisation, conformity assessment, examination procedures, and the marks themselves. The results underscore the complex nature of the issues involved and highlight the need to find ways to lessen the opportunities for product safety standards and conformity assessment requirements to become barriers to trade.

A review of the surveys reveals certain differences in the way safety agencies and manufacturers view product safety standards and conformity assessment procedures. For manufacturers and their trade associations, issues involving product safety standards and conformity assessment requirements are becoming more important as global competition intensifies. Safety agencies appear to have a different focus, concentrating on the effects of national or regional product safety standards and conformity assessment requirements on consumer safety. Perhaps as a consequence, the responses from safety agencies were inclined to emphasise similarities among different product safety standards and to minimise the effort needed to comply with conformity assessment procedures.

On the other hand, manufacturers and trade associations, which actively participate in the global market, tend to focus on the differences among product safety standards and on the burdens of conformity assessment procedures. Insignificant variations in product standards, which have no effect on a product's inherent safety, can create costly production difficulties according to manufacturers. Moreover, for a manufacturer who sells in several countries, national and regional conformity assessment requirements that result in the duplicative re-testing of products are a major concern. According to manufacturers and trade associations, it is difficult to justify the costly and time-consuming duplicative testing of products in a highly competitive environment. From a consumer perspective, this can mean higher prices and restricted choice, with no substantial improvement in product safety.

Essentially, the difference in the point of view of safety agencies and manufacturers is reflected in data which reflects contradictory characterisation of the same product standards. Frequently, product standards that safety agencies characterise as voluntary, manufacturers would call mandatory. While in theory there should be no question about whether a standard is voluntary or mandatory, in practice such distinctions apparently become less clear. Differences in the points of view of safety agencies and manufacturers may lessen as issues involving product safety standards and conformity assessment requirements are addressed in the context of international trade. But despite positive signs that the movement in that direction has begun, differences remain.

With respect to product safety standards for the four products surveyed, safety agencies indicated that national or regional safety standards are often equivalent to international or quasi-international standards. The survey indicated that this is especially true with respect to national and regional microwave oven standards, which appear to be largely equivalent to IEC standards. Moreover, safety agency responses also indicated that there is an ISO standard for petrol-driven lawn mowers; and electric lawn mowers standards are generally equivalent to the IEC standards. In the product category of toys, the responses from safety agencies suggested that national standards are often equivalent to quasi-international standards, i.e. ASTM and CEN standards. At the same time, they indicated that an ISO toy standard is under development. While standardisation is relatively new to bicycle helmets, there are suggestions that bicycle helmet standards development is moving in the direction of equivalency with other standards.

The responses from manufacturers, however, stressed existing differences among product safety standards for the four products. The majority of responding manufacturers believe that current standards increase the cost of their products and agree that the standards create delays in placing new products on the market. The strength of this attitude toward product safety standards varies to some degree depending on the product. Product safety standards for microwave ovens, which do not differ substantially from country to country, are viewed positively. Product safety standards for toys, on the other hand, often differ and seem to be a source of dissatisfaction. In addition to the standards themselves, there is some dissatisfaction with the standardisation processes. In particular, North American respondents often protested about being excluded from the CEN standardisation process and object to the Vienna Agreement. They believe that there is a pressing need to harmonise the product safety standards for these products by eliminating any differences so that their products can satisfy the provisions of one international standard.

Manufacturers and trade associations are equally concerned with current conformity assessment practices. Differing conformity assessment requirements, like differing product safety standards, add costs with no increase in product safety are of great concern to those competing in a global marketplace. Manufacturers and trade associations would like to see the establishment of mechanisms that would permit greater use of manufacturer's self-declaration of conformance and, where pre-market governmental approval is required, the mutual recognition of testing results and certificates. In particular, they appear to share the belief that it should only be necessary to test a product once and that those results should be accepted world-wide.

The mutual recognition of conformity assessment results appears to have achieved a certain level of acceptance among OECD Member countries, according to the responses from Delegates. Their responses indicate that such agreements exist in several contexts. Obviously, the most prominent mutual recognition agreement with respect to certification results is in the European Union. The results of any EU notified body for a particular product must be accepted in any EU country. However, this particular arrangement has created difficulty with non-EU countries who would like to see greater acceptance of certification results from outside of the European Union, as well as greater use of manufacturers' declarations of conformance and less use of third-party testing if it is not cost effective.

Outside of the European Union, mutual recognition agreements are less common but they exist. Mexico and Turkey have entered into mutual recognition agreements with many countries. Japan has mechanisms which allow for the acceptance of foreign testing, but not certification results in certain instances in the regulatory sphere. Japan and others indicated in their responses that in the case of microwave ovens they accept the results of testing bodies that are members of the IECEE-CB system. While toy manufacturers in Japan do not have to be registered with the government in order to market their products, manufacturers of microwave ovens and electric lawn mowers must be registered as well as meet other mandatory requirements before being permitted to place their products on the market. With respect to the United States, there are no federal restrictions concerning the acceptance of results. Private contracts between the manufacturer and distributor/importer, however, may specify the kind of testing and certification required.

In summary, the nature of product safety standardisation and conformity assessment requirements, which are often product specific, makes generalisations difficult. However, it is possible to draw certain conclusions from the survey data:

-- product safety standards and conformity assessment procedures are acknowledged to be among some of the most important trade issues today and are becoming more critical as the global marketplace develops;

-- manufacturers and trade associations have a strong interest in having these issues addressed. They believe it is necessary to eliminate differences in product safety standards and promote mutual recognition of testing and certification results. Ideally manufacturers and trade associations would like to contend with one international safety standard, one international testing and certification procedure, and one international safety mark;

-- consumers have a strong interest in participating in the global marketplace and knowing with confidence that the products sold there are safe. It is in the consumer interest to ensure that the means of maintaining or increasing product safety do not lead to higher costs and reduced selection;

-- safety agencies are beginning to consider product safety standards and conformity assessment requirements in the context of international trade, and some have suggested that there may be no contradiction between consumer interest and reducing barriers to trade. In fact, as the common interests of the manufacturer and the consumer become clearer, the solution to many of the issues involving product safety standards and conformity assessment may become more apparent;

-- in the interest of regulatory efficiency, the burden of conformity assessment requirements should be subjected to a more rigorous cost-benefit analysis in order to best deploy increasingly limited public resources;

-- survey data suggests that small- and medium-sized manufacturers may be at a competitive disadvantage in satisfying standard and conformity assessment criteria;

-- despite increasing interest in this area, the survey suggests widespread confusion in the definition and characterisation of certain basic terminology and concepts.

Part III

SPEAKERS' REMARKS FROM THE 1995 OECD CONFERENCE ON CONSUMER PRODUCT SAFETY STANDARDS AND CONFORMITY ASSESSMENTS: THEIR EFFECT ON INTERNATIONAL TRADE

OPENING SESSION

Keynote address

Mr. Jesús SEADE
Deputy Director-General
World Trade Organisation,
Switzerland

Opening remarks

Mr. Nils RINGSTEDT
Conference Chairman
Vice Chairman - OECD Committee on Consumer Policy
Chairman of the Working Party on Consumer Safety
Deputy Director-General
National Swedish Board for Consumer Policies,
Sweden

Mr. Christian BABUSIAUX
Director-General, Directorate General on Competition,
Consumer Affairs and Fraud Repression,
France

Mr. Lyn HANSEN
Director, Safety Policy
Federal Bureau of Consumer Affairs,
Australia

Keynote address[56]

Jesús SEADE

Introduction

As part of the "Cecchini Report," a survey was undertaken of eleven thousand business leaders in the European Communities who were asked to rank the importance of national standards and regulations, along with seven other general categories of trade impediments,[57] as a hindrance to intra-Community trade. In four major EC countries, business leaders ranked divergent national standards and regulations, in other words "technical barriers to trade" (or TBTs for short), *at the top* of their list of internal market barriers. The EC-wide average of all responses placed TBTs as the *second* most important obstacle to intra-Community trade.

I think we can safely presume that, if TBTs are a significant trade problem within the relatively homogenous and tightly-knit group of countries that form the European Community, it is likely to be a bigger problem in other less homogenous regions of the world, and particularly in trade *between* regions, even if I cannot substantiate this claim with numbers because of difficulties in gathering evidence in this area. Unfortunately, assessing the trade effects of TBTs is far more difficult than assessing the impact of "regular" trade barriers. The effects of tariffs, for example, can be assessed in simple economic models using price and volume data in conjunction with estimates of the various elasticities. By contrast, the effects of technical barriers are much more demanding to assess, both in terms of theory and data requirements, as they depend on firm-specific costs of adapting products to different markets, the cost and delays of certification itself, the loss of scale-economies in production, the excessive storage cost as units produced for one market cannot be redirected to other markets without modifications, and so forth.

Lacking "hard" statistical evidence, much of what we know about the significance of technical barriers is by anecdote and example. The same holds true for the effects of "conformity assessment," where systematic evidence seems even more scant. This makes the survey launched by the OECD Committee on Consumer Policy extremely valuable, and I would like to commend the Committee members for their initiative. But let me briefly review some trade aspects of the debate over technical barriers, and the way the problem is approached in the new WTO Agreement on TBTs. (A more detailed presentation of the WTO agreement will be provided in Panel IV of this Conference by the WTO expert in this area, Mrs. Vivien Liu.)

Technical Barriers to Trade

It is somewhat ironic that product standards and regulations sometimes *create* trade barriers, as many of them evolved for the opposite purpose of *facilitating* trade. For example, standardised weights and measures were developed centuries and millennia ago to facilitate commerce and obviate the problem of fraud. The coinage of silver and gold is another example. Seen from today's perspective, the problem with these early standardisation efforts was that they took place within limited geographical areas, and as a consequence often left a heritage of deeply-rooted competing standards, for example and rather pervasively with the "imperial" and the "metric" systems of weights and measures.

While it may be too late or too costly to act upon historical differences today, there is no need to repeat the mistakes of yesterday. But please do not misunderstand me on this point: some differences in standards are quite legitimate. For example, there may be genuine differences in risk-tolerance among countries, in particular but not exclusively among nations at different stages of economic development. Countries may also interpret scientific evidence in different ways. One example is the dispute between the United States and the European Community regarding the EC's ban on imports of meat treated with growth hormones, where the United States argues that there is no evidence of health risk for humans while the European Community maintains that 100 per cent safety has not been scientifically established.

On the other hand, we should not be ignorant of the fact that standards and regulations can be *deliberately* drafted to protect the domestic industry from international competition, and so can the procedures for assessing conformity with standards and regulations. Let me give you a few examples.

A famous case involved the "pasta purity" regulations in Italy, which for many years prohibited the sale of any product labelled "pasta" that was not made *entirely* from durum wheat. As it happens, durum wheat is grown extensively in Southern Italy but not much elsewhere in Europe. The sale of imported pasta -- excuse me, "pasta-like" products -- fell to almost nothing after the introduction of the "pasta purity" regulation scaring away consumers from products they previously accepted as pasta. A similar case is that of the German "beer purity" regulations, precluding the sale of any product labelled "beer" that contained ingredients not used in the German brewing tradition. Regulations of this type often seek to protect consumers from deception or confusion. There is no doubt this is a worthwhile objective, but it is also one which lends itself to protectionist abuse.

In all this I have been referring to standards and regulations quite indistinctly. This is intentional. Sure enough, standards are "voluntary" while regulations are "mandatory." However, standards tend to become mandatory in *practice* in many cases, something which is also confirmed by the OECD survey. Compliance with standards is often "encouraged," to say the least, by insurers and insurance underwriters; and then they may become virtually mandatory in practice through the resistance of *consumers* to buy products without certain labels. For example, the market penetration of European and American skis in Japan was not very good for a long time, as they were not thick enough to be eligible for the Japanese seal of approval for those products. The case was amicably solved in the early stage of dispute resolution under the GATT, as Japan accepted that its argument for diverging from the existing international standard on the issue -- that "Japanese snow is different" -- did not cut a lot of ice.[58]

Examples like these, and the fact that firms in most cases seem willing to incur the cost of getting a seal of approval, indicate that standards are perceived as mandatory in many cases. The similarity between the "voluntariness" of standards and the "voluntariness" of so-called "voluntary export restraints" is striking in this regard. Both are "voluntary" in theory but mandatory in practice. Alongside the need for conformity to foreign standards and regulations, is the fact and burden of *demonstrating* this conformity, which in itself can become a trade obstacle.

Legal Obligations

Let me now outline our main GATT and WTO legal provisions where they bear on technical barriers and conformity assessments.

The original GATT agreement of 1947 did not address technical barriers separately, which were treated in conjunction with other non-tariff barriers and subject to the same disciplines and exceptions. A key provision is that of *national treatment* under Article III requiring treatment no less favourable than that accorded to like products of national origin. A domestic law requiring, for example, imports to undergo a greater number of safety tests *may* run afoul of this principle.

However, certain exceptions exist that somewhat weaken this obligation. Subject to the requirement that such measures are not applied in a manner which would constitute a means of arbitrary or unjustifiable discrimination between countries, or a disguised restriction on international trade, Article XX(b) exempts measures "*necessary* to protect human, animal, or plant life and health," and Article XX(d) exempts measures "*necessary* to the prevention of deceptive practices."

The limitations of the General Agreement led to an initiative during the Tokyo Round negotiations at the end of the 70s to develop new obligations regarding technical barriers, culminating in a plurilateral side-agreement to GATT, known as the Standard Code. While the signing of this side-agreement was voluntary, and thereby applied only to signatories, most of the larger trading nations, with the notable exception of Australia, signed on. It came into effect in January 1980.

I will not go into the details of this agreement, since it in large part overlaps with the new WTO Agreement on Technical Barriers to Trade, which I will discuss in some detail in a moment. Let me just note that a key provision of the code provided that "where technical regulations or standards are required and relevant international standards exist or their completion is imminent, Parties *shall* use them, or relevant parts of them except where, as duly explained upon request, such international standards or relevant parts are inappropriate for the Parties concerned." A non-exhaustive list of reasons why international standards might be inappropriate included *(i)* the prevention of deceptive practices; *(ii)* protection of human health or safety, animal or plant life or health, or the environment; *(iii)* fundamental climate or other geographical factors; and (iv) fundamental technological problems.

Countries were requested to notify proposed standards and regulations in advance, to give other Parties time to react and adapt, if they were not based in whole or in part on international standards and if they "may have a *significant* effect on trade of other Parties." Between 1980 and the end of 1994, the GATT Secretariat received a total of some 5 000 such notifications. While these reported numbers are important, the *actual* number of national standards adopted is quite unknown to us, in particular because the obligation to notify only applies where those standards and regulations are deemed to have a *significant* effect on the trade of other Partners, which in practice is subjective and hard to tell.

If we now look at the objective, or reasons, stated by governments for the adoption of divergent national standards over the 1980-1994 period, the composition looks as follows.[59] Almost 50 per cent of the cases, or 47.4 per cent to be exact, were motivated for "human health and safety" reasons. That is, international standards, to the extent they existed, were considered to be inappropriate. The *second* largest group, comprising somewhat more than 15.6 per cent of the cases, refer to "quality requirements." This group consists of technical requirements and regulations that are related to performance requirements and quality aspects of a product. Here, one also finds quality and production control and, furthermore, certification and testing requirements. The *third* largest group, comprising some nine per cent of the cases, refers to measures for the "prevention of deceptive practices," including labelling requirements, packaging requirements, and requirements on measurements (size, weights, etc.). The heading harmonisation and standards, with virtually the same share, refers mainly to cases of *regional* harmonisation and standardisation, for example, when the members states of the European Community have gone from national to EC-wide standards. The *fifth* largest group, comprising some *eight* per cent of the cases, relates to national "environmental" standards. *Finally*, the heading "other" included a host of miscellaneous reasons, such as national security, and protection of the life or health of animals or plants.

Let me now turn to the WTO Agreement on Technical Barriers to Trade, which came into effect in January of this year. In contrast to the Tokyo Round Standard Code, the new agreement, first of all, covers *all* WTO Members and not just those countries that subscribed to the Tokyo Round agreement. If you like, the standards regarding standards and regulations, and including conformity assessment procedures, have now been standardised. That must be music to the ears of a standardiser?

So what are the main provisions of the new agreement? First, regarding coverage, because agricultural issues are so contentious, and specific too, it was decided to negotiate a free-standing agreement on Sanitary and Phytosanitary Measures, while other technical barriers, except those relating to Government Procurement, are covered by the new Agreement on Technical Barriers to Trade. I will only talk about the latter here.

The new TBT agreement expands and refines many of the obligations of the Tokyo Round Standard Codes. The agreement includes the basic non-discriminatory principles found in virtually all agreements of the WTO, namely, the most favoured nation and the national treatment principles. These are well known and I shall not dwell on them here. As with the Tokyo Round code, international standards, or the relevant parts of them, *shall* be used, except when they "would be an ineffective or inappropriate means for the fulfilment of the legitimate objective pursued, for instance because of fundamental climatic or geographical factors or fundamental technological problems" (Article 2.4).

Interestingly, some of the wording of Article 2, paragraphs 2 to 5, suggests that the obligation to use international standards extends to *pre-existing* regulations, not just new ones, and, moreover, that technical regulations shall *not be more trade restrictive than necessary*.[60] A guideline in this respect is given in Article 2.8: "Wherever appropriate, Members shall specify technical regulations in terms of *performance* rather than design or descriptive characteristics." Thus, if the regulators are concerned with, for example, the strength of skis, they should specify the strength requirements rather than how thick they have to be. Such an approach is preferable because it permits product development in a greater way than design requirements do. Another related guideline is, as expressed in Article 2.7, that "Members shall give positive consideration to accepting as equivalent technical regulations of other Members, even if these regulations differ from their own, provided that they are satisfied that these regulations adequately fulfil the objectives of their own regulations." Also, as in the Tokyo Round Code, Members are requested to notify at an appropriate early stage technical regulations that diverge from international standards and that may have a *significant* effect on trade.

Let me now turn to the rules pertinent to *procedures* for the assessment of conformity by central government bodies. Once again, the most favoured nation and the national treatment principles apply: discrimination against foreign exporters seeking to certify their products for sale in your market is absolutely forbidden. Moreover, a less restrictive rule also applies: As expressed in Article 5.1.2: "conformity assessment procedures are not prepared, adopted or applied with a view to or with the effect of creating unnecessary obstacles to international trade. This means, *inter alia*, that conformity assessment procedures shall not be more strict or be applied more strictly than is necessary to give the importing Member adequate confidence that products conform with the applicable technical regulations or standards, taking account of the risks non-conformity would create."

Another very interesting provision is that Members are "encouraged" to pursue negotiations towards agreements on "mutual recognition of (test) results." This would allow exporters to assess conformity at home and only once, instead of having to do so in each and every export market that they wish to pursue, which presumably would save much time and costs – to them and to consumers. However, it may be a long time before this becomes a global reality. Countries have to first gain confidence in each others' testing and certification procedures. However, one could imagine a development, which I believe has already started, where countries accredit each others' certification *bodies*, rather than certifying each others' *products*.

Another area that could see improvements is the fact that the rules formally apply only to Central Government Bodies, whereas much of the standardisation and conformity- assessment activities may take place at the local government level or by private bodies. However, Members are requested to take such reasonable measures as may be available to them to ensure the compliance of local and non-governmental bodies, and to try to get them to accept and comply with the Code of Good Practice for the Preparation, Adoption and Application of Standards in Annex 3 to the TBT Agreement. Only 23 bodies, including central government bodies for whom the Code is mandatory, had notified the signing of the Code of Good Practice by the end of November, 1995. This is somewhat disappointing, given that there are hundreds of standardisation bodies in the world. I would encourage this assembly to work for comprehensive coverage in this area.

Conclusion

To conclude, the new WTO Agreement on Technical Barriers to Trade provides a legal framework for the work of standardising and conformity assessment bodies around the world. The rules are enforceable through our new Dispute Settlement provisions and procedures that form part of the WTO Agreement. As is well known, these procedures mark a substantial change from the past. They are a unified set of rules which apply generally to all WTO disputes, the adoption of panel reports cannot be blocked by parties to the dispute, and they provide for the appeal of a panel decision to a new, seven-person Appellate Body.

Out of the 21 requests for consultation received under the new WTO Agreements in the course of this year -- consultation being the first step of our adjudication process -- seven cases, that is a *third* of them, involve TBTs in one way or another. This suggest two things. *First*, technical barriers continue to be an area susceptible to protectionist abuse. And *second*, countries who see their trade privileges being compromised, are now seizing the opportunity to use the TBT agreement to enforce their rights. This is a good sign for the future.

Opening remarks

Nils RINGSTEDT

On behalf of the OECD Committee on Consumer Policy, I wish you all a very warm welcome to the Conference on Consumer Product Safety Standards and Conformity Assessment: Their Effect on International Trade. This conference is taking place at a milestone for the Committee: yesterday we concluded the 50th meeting of the Committee on Consumer Policy. To me, this is of particular importance, because I have had the privilege of being a Delegate to the Committee from almost the very beginning, and I have had the pleasure of chairing the Working Party on Consumer Safety since 1981. During this period, the Working Party has taken up a variety of product safety issues and has certainly influenced the direction of consumer safety policy in Member countries.

Consumer safety issues and their impact on international trade has been a permanent item on the Agenda of our Committee. Safety standards and conformity assessment, in particular, play an important role in this context. They are probably the most important part of any national consumer safety policy because they establish and ensure a basic safety level for consumer products available on the market.

However, we also know that the proliferation of national safety rules and standards can interrupt the free movement of goods. This is why the Committee examined the role of the safety standards in this respect in a 1991 report entitled "Consumers, Product Safety Standards and International Trade." The report discussed the development of standards at the national, regional and international level and their impact on trade. It identified problems associated with monitoring compliance with standards and related issues of certification, and concluded with a number of recommendations including the following: "Relevant intergovernmental and non-governmental organisations should increase their co-operation in the area of product safety with a view to defining criteria for mutual recognition of standards, certification procedures and test methods."

The importance of standardisation and conformity assessment issues has grown enormously during recent years, both regionally -- in particular in Europe -- and now, globally. The Committee therefore decided to follow up on the 1991 report in order to study in greater detail the operation of product safety standards and conformity assessment requirements and their impact on consumers and international trade, and to look for ways in which governments can facilitate trade in safe consumer products.

Since there was very little information on the practical aspects of these issues, we decided to examine them on the basis of a number of case studies i.e. consumer products that were internationally traded and subject to safety requirements. This included a questionnaire enquiry to better understand the development of safety standards, the manufacturing of the goods, and the conformity assessment process until, finally, the product enters domestic or foreign markets. While the emphasis of the fact-finding aspects of the study have been on the practical problems identified by firms that manufacture and sell consumer products for export, the final goal is to ensure that consumers reap the benefits of open markets with the confidence that the products they find there are safe. The Committee selected four product areas for study after consultations with exporters i.e. toys, lawn mowers, microwave ovens and bicycle helmets. Also, when designing this study, we were concerned about the problems -- if any -- for small- and medium-sized firms in participating in the global market and, in particular, we were interested in the impact of the standardisation and conformity assessment processes on them.

The initial phase of the study also included a survey undertaken by the OECD Secretariat to gather basic information from Member government agencies concerning safety standards and conformity assessment requirements in the four product areas. Following the survey of government safety agencies, the next phase of the study involved the distribution of three separate questionnaires to manufacturers, trade associations and standards and conformity assessment bodies.

Before concluding these introductory remarks, a few words about what we hope to achieve. In summary, the aim of the conference is to:

-- provide an overview of the existing national, regional and international framework for product standardisation and conformity assessment;

-- show the operation of accreditation, mutual recognition and testing requirements at the national and regional level;

-- give the parties involved in these procedures, such as governmental safety agencies, standardising bodies, testing laboratories, exporters and consumer bodies, an opportunity to express their views on the functioning of the system in practice; and

-- consider the ways and means for improving the current situation.

The Committee on Consumer Policy sees this meeting as *a fact-finding conference*. We therefore hope to have a lively discussion in each panel session, with concrete examples and with participation from all of you in the audience! With these introductory words, I invite Mr. Babusiaux of the French Directorate General on Competition, Consumer Affairs and Fraud Repression to present his opening remarks.

Christian BABUSIAUX

The Directorate in France for which I am responsible has as its mission the opening of the market to competition, the supervision of market transactions, the protection of consumers, and the control of quality and product safety. I think there is a link between all these topics, and Directorates such as mine play an important role in ensuring a satisfactory functioning of the market in OECD countries.

I think we all believe in the importance of having an open international market. But this market must work in a correct way, without any exaggerated barriers and without any safety problems for consumers. We have to make a synthesis between all these important concerns. Companies and consumers will all gain benefits from international trade, which provides access to broader markets, and to more diverse products at lower prices. But we have to examine how this international trade should best be conducted.

There are standards in each of our countries and it is obvious that if there are differences between those standards, there will be potential barriers to trade. But we can not eliminate all standards and regulations, because that would present a serious problem for consumer safety. We therefore have to reconcile the different requirements in this area. Personally, I see three directions for potential improvements in this field.

The first direction for all of us would be to continue improving standard harmonisation. I believe that this is an important action, but it is clearly very difficult as we all know, because it can take decades to harmonise rules. The work of the European Union in this area gives us an opportunity to assess the difficulty of the work, but these difficulties should not force us to give up this effort, neither within the European Union nor within a broader international framework. There is a standardisation body at the global level, and I would say that any publication of an international standard is an important improvement.

But it is also obvious that harmonisation cannot be the only means. It is extremely difficult and, in a certain number of cases, standards are different because they reflect the state of our societies, each of which has distinct customs, requirements, levels of consumption, etc. Thus standards will by nature retain certain differences.

Therefore, we must seek to discover commonalties, and based on these create convergence between each country's regulations. We must seek this convergence particularly for safety rules, because I think that on the safety problem, the requirements in our different countries are closer to one another than in the area of quality problems. Specifically, I mean that the level of risk can be more easily compared in our different countries, while the quality notion is much more subjective and is more a response to cultural habits. So, we have to go as far as possible, as quickly as possible, in the convergence of rules in the field of safety. Then, we have to develop consumer information on products because rules are different in each country. This difference is not illegitimate, and it is important for the consumer to have the opportunity to assess a product's qualities and how it differs from similar products. That is why we need qualitative information on products included in the packaging and labelling. This is important because today consumers are better informed and aware, and can choose themselves between products provided they that have enough information.

The second direction is by the establishment and maintenance of a control system in each country which facilitates the comparison of different testing systems' performances, in a move toward mutual recognition of the tests made in different countries. Of course, manufacturers are primarily responsible for the products' quality and safety. In many countries, including France, but also since a recent Directive, in all countries of the European Union, the manufacturer is required to ensure the safety of the products he launches on the market. While this is of course an important principle, each State should be entitled to establish a second-level control system, set up by public control bodies, because each of our States is also responsible for the safety and quality of products on the market. If we don't want standards to be artificial barriers to trade hidden under the guise of controls, there must be a sufficient level of mutual confidence between the different institutions involved.

But in order to have this level of confidence, some conditions must be fulfilled. We need sufficient controls in our countries to achieve the possibility of mutual recognition. In our OECD countries, in general, there is a good control level because our consumers believe it is extremely important. But we know that is not the case in every country of the world, and therefore we find non-conforming products in our national markets even if we try to prevent them from entering our territories. The presence of these products is bad for the consumer and has a negative effect on the functioning of international trade.

For this reason, we should dedicate greater attention to achieving greater levels of confidence in products imported from non-OECD countries as well.

As to controls on food products, we have carried out work under the aegis of Codex Alimentarius, which is the world organisation for standards on food products. Within the framework of Codex, a working group on standardisation of the control systems of the different countries has been established to propel us towards a global accreditation of control systems. Considering the importance of industrial standards in international trade, we must eventually consider the daunting task of global accreditation in this area as well.

The third path for improvement is the development of increased international co-operation. Indeed, national systems must not only be equivalent, but they also must co-operate, exchange information and adopt similar control methods. This is important because we know that even when standards can be compared, we still have to interpret those standards. Therefore co-operation is required to ensure that interpretation is equivalent in the different States. Within the OECD, there has been a notification process on dangerous products for many years. I think this network is positive but it could also work in a more active way, and it is perhaps time to examine how to modernise the functioning of this network in the interests of our companies and consumers. We would thus create, between the OECD countries, a network for monitoring deceptive practices and defective products. It could function in an informal way, but would link OECD member States and would be a great help in this area.

These are just a few suggestions for new directions in this area. The issues to which the conference is dedicated are very important to French companies and consumers. You can be certain French authorities will devote great attention to the results of this work, and I hope that it will be the same for your countries' authorities. We are all facing the same kinds of problems, so it is important to try to find a way to solve them together.

Lyn HANSEN

We are here to discuss the problems and the opportunities arising from the globalisation of consumer markets. There are many important issues that each of us must address if we are to participate effectively in the international economy. Of course, the focus of this conference is on product safety and conformity to national standards in an increasingly free trade environment. It will also concern how we tackle regulations when assisting domestic industries to access global market places while, at the same time, ensuring that consumers have access to safe products.

Many of us have already been looking hard at solutions such as conformity assessment, certification, and mutual recognition agreements as a means of overcoming some of the potential problems. These are areas which will receive further exploration over the next two days.

Product safety is integral to the market place. Safety should be a key consideration for the principal players in the market place: consumers, business, industry and government. If we fail in protecting consumers from unsafe products, then we fail in the marketplace overall. The liberalisation of internal and external markets has made it imperative for all these players to develop a new outlook on product safety. Obviously, different countries have different rules and regulations, and often, even a different outlook on how best to protect their consumers in both the domestic and the global market place. That is why it is so important that we gather under the umbrella of the OECD to share our ideas and experiences in the hope that we can determine compatible solutions where necessary.

Australian governments and Australian industry have committed themselves to become internationally competitive. There have already been major structural changes undertaken by government and industries in removing restrictive protection barriers, and we have become much more aggressive in our export strategies. The challenge for us now, as for all of you, is to come up with the means by which we can balance trade liberalisation and product safety. The Australian government is committed to creating a culture of safety in the market place. If we are successful in creating a culture of safety, it will be possible to free business from the excessive regulatory constraints and encourage it to incorporate safety in its commercial decisions. The culture of safety will require consumers as well as business to be involved in a transparent decision making process about product safety policy.

The reforms proposed will create an innovative, flexible, and above all relevant product safety infrastructure and thus reinforce the commitment of government to consumer protection. While the Australian government is certainly interested in Australia's future in the global economy, it has also signed up, as has many other OECD country members, to the Asia-Pacific Economic Co-operation Agreement, which is committing the Australia/Pacific region to eliminating trade barriers by the year 2020. As a member of both of these organisations, Australia is in the unique position of being able to develop a product safety culture which applies to the entire region, but only if we act quickly enough.

It was about this time last year that the Australian Federal Minister of Consumer Affairs, Janet McHugh, visited the Consumer Safety Institute in Holland and met with its Executive Director, Dr. Wim Rogmans. As a result, the Minister took home to the Australian government a plan to adopt a similar approach to the setting of mandatory standards, as is currently explored in Europe. The plan involves a new approach to the process of standard-setting which turns on its head the present methodology.

Over the past 20 years, the Commonwealth, state and territory governments in Australia have developed a detailed regulatory framework for prescribing product safety and information standards and for banning unsafe goods. This infrastructure has been criticised as being too complex, inconsistent and imposing significant costs on business and thereby on consumers. The prescriptive regime has impeded not only innovations by Australian manufacturers, but also their ability to take advantage of greater access to export markets. There have been concerns about the time it takes to introduce mandatory standards, and the absence of any co-ordinated consideration of what hazard-reducing outcome a standard is meant to achieve. For example, it can currently take up to four years to develop a mandatory safety standard in Australia and there are presently only 18 in existence. These standards apply to individual products aimed at a particular product group such as helmets. However, the method being explored in Europe and which the government would like to see implemented in Australia focuses on performance standards that apply to the potential hazard rather than to the individual product. They are horizontal rather than vertical. The Minister would like to see this process adopted in line with the APEC Agreement so that Australia can set the scene for product safety in the region. The Australian government is also conscious of the need to be consistent with the international markets if Australian and other businesses are to enjoy the benefits of international trade.

All Australian governments, commonwealth, states and territories, could, for instance, amend the Consumer Protection Acts to incorporate a general safety provision along the lines of that introduced by the European Union. Such a provision could set a basic level to maintain existing quality and safety without direct interference of governments. Instead, it places the obligation on all those involved in the supply chain to take the necessary steps to ensure that the product is safe. The obligation of safety should rightly be with those in the supply chain.

Responsibility for the design and construction of a product is with the producer and should not be set by governments. However, governments should be prepared to step in if things go wrong. Such a model has the potential of being adopted on a regional basis and could be a useful instrument for the APEC Agreement.

Another area for investigation is the development of a single recognisable certification mark which may be the best way for consumers to ensure that they can distinguish between those products which meet standards and those which do not. A certification mark could indicate compliance with a voluntary or a mandatory consumer safety standard, and foster market transparency and equity. This would give consumers information that the standard has been adhered to and give business the opportunity to promote the safety and quality of their products. Certainly, in Australia at least, there have already been fears among some groups, and within the consumer movement itself, about the potential for safety standards to take a back seat under any new free trade agreements. There have been many reports suggesting that free trade would enable and indeed encourage the dumping of inferior unsafe products onto Australian shores. This, of course, will not happen if governments, business, industry and consumers work together to ensure that a culture of safety is developed within Australia and within our region as a matter of priority. The Australian government is committed to achieving the trade liberalisation goals for the Asia-Pacific region as agreed by the Bogor declaration last year.

A key to achieving this is through the removal of unnecessary technical barriers to trade such as those arising from overly prescriptive product safety standards. As I mentioned earlier, Australia is already working on initiatives to develop performance-based safety standards to ensure that consumers and business have the best available information on which to make decisions about product safety. The Minister's Department is directly involved as chair of an expert working group of APEC representatives in developing a mutual recognition agreement on conformity assessment for toys. This is a pilot project aimed at providing both a working agreement for toy products as well as providing a model for future agreements.

In Australia, we have recognised the need to foster a new culture in our national market place which makes safety a key consideration in the decision of consumers and suppliers, and which removes the need for restrictive regulatory structures by government. This is a way we can ensure that product safety remains integral to the market place, and that consumers enjoy one of their basic rights, which is the right to safe products in the market, be they domestic or international.

Panel I

STANDARDISATION, CERTIFICATION AND PRODUCT SAFETY IN A GLOBAL MARKET

Chairman

Mr. Sergio MAZZA
President
American National Standards Institute (ANSI)
United States

Summary of Remarks

Panellists

Mr. Bruce J. FARQUHAR
Acting Secretary-General
European Association for the Co-ordination of Consumer Representation in Standardisation
Belgium

Mr. Bernard VAUCELLE
Director General
Association Française de Normalisation (AFNOR)
France

Mr. David MILLER
President
Toy Manufacturers of America
United States

Mr. Jürgen NEUN
Technical Director Conformity Assessment
Deutsches Institut für Normung e.V. (DIN)
Germany

Product safety policy has been greatly influenced in the past few years by a growing number of both regional and global initiatives aimed principally at promoting the greater liberalisation of international trade. These developments have had considerable consequences for the implementation of product safety policy. Most importantly, they have given rise to a greater demand for the use of international standards and for the mutual recognition of conformity assessment procedures.

The role of standardisation as an important tool in the elimination of technical barriers of trade was recognised more than fifteen years ago, and formed the foundation of the New Approach to technical harmonisation in the European Union. The relative success of the New Approach has led to an acknowledgement of the positive role standards can play in eliminating technical barriers to trade. This has resulted in a specific reference to the use of international standards being made in the recently completed revised GATT agreement on technical barriers to trade.

Following the considerable discussion that has surrounded the elimination of technical barriers to trade resulting from differing technical specifications, the spotlight is beginning to fall upon the conformity assessment procedures that have to be applied to products before they can gain access to markets. Multiple testing of the same product can lead to enormous costs being added to the production of a product, costs which are ultimately passed on to the consumer and which may not provide any benefit whatsoever in terms of increased levels of safety.

Europe has led the way with the establishment of a global approach to conformity assessment. This is meant to provide a structure which will allow the mutual recognition of test results and certification within the single market. One recent initiative to further these objectives has been the establishment of the Keymark, a joint CEN/CENELEC mark of conformity to European standards.

At the international level, initiatives are being launched concerning the mutual recognition of accreditation of quality management systems (ISO-QSAR) and of electronic components (IEC-EE). Attention is also being given to mutual recognition agreements under the auspices of different regional trading agreements such as NAFTA, ASEAN and MERCOSUR and as a result of increased transatlantic business dialogue.

Against this backdrop of fundamental change a number of concerns have been expressed by consumer organisations which threaten to undermine consumer confidence in the market place, and have potentially serious adverse consequences for the cause of free trade.

Consumers have, for example, been concerned over the perceived dangers surrounding harmonisation at an ever higher level and involving more and more countries. The fear is always that the pressures associated with such a process will lead to harmonisation at the level of the lowest common denominator. Experience in Europe has shown us that this need not necessarily be the case, with in fact many new European standards greatly advancing consumer safety in certain areas. The international standards bodies may however face a greater challenge in trying to resolve the demands of the industrialised world with those of the developing countries.

The dumping of dangerous products onto markets where perhaps enforcement and control is less well developed is another major issue. This happens not only in developing countries, but also in the central and eastern European countries where demand for western-style goods has increased dramatically, and even within the European Union itself. Counterfeiting of products such as automobile spare parts and medicines also poses a serious problem.

Standards bodies and national administrations have to examine how they can adapt their policies and structures to take account of the new pressures. Transparency in the standards-setting process will be a pre-requisite to consumer acceptance of standards. National administrations will need to greatly increase the level of international co-operation to ensure uniform enforcement in an increasingly international market-place. The integrity of conformity assessment schemes will also be critical to consumer confidence in the market-place, and the activities of testing houses under mutual recognition agreements will need to be scrutinised to ensure consistency.

The consumer movement also has to deal with these changes in domestic and international markets. In particular the challenge for consumers has been to respond to this shift in emphasis away from the use of detailed technical specifications in legislation to the more widespread use of standards and greater liberalisation in the recognition of the results of conformity assessment procedures. Consequently, consumers are becoming more actively involved in the work of the standards bodies. Previously the work of the standards bodies has been dominated by industrial interests, but the need for direct participation of all the economic and social partners has been acknowledged at the highest political levels. For example, the European Council has taken a number of resolutions dealing with the need for an open transparent process, and the European Commission has gone as far as to declare that the active participation of social and economic partners at every level in standardisation is a political pre-condition to the further development of European standardisation.

While consumer representation in standardisation is well-established in many countries with, for example, long standing national consumer standardisation councils in the United Kingdom, Germany, France and the United States, and considerable progress has been made in the past few years, much has still to be done. Furthermore, the shift in emphasis away from national standardisation activities towards regional and international standardisation has necessitated the development of structures to ensure co-ordination of national consumer input and, where necessary, direct consumer representation at the regional or international level.

At the international level, direct consumer participation in technical committees and working groups can be achieved through Consumers International (CI, formerly IOCU -- the International Organisation of Consumers Unions) which has liaison status with the international standards bodies IEC and ISO. CI furthermore tries to co-ordinate the representation activities of its many members who are the independent national consumer organisations in over 100 countries world-wide. CI also participates in the work of COPOLCO, the ISO Consumer Policy Committee, which is made up of delegations from ISO's national members.

At the European level, the need to have a single consumer voice, especially at the political level, has long been recognised. It was not, however, until earlier this year that ANEC, the new European association for the co-ordination of consumer representation in standardisation, was established. ANEC members are nominated by independent national consumer organisations from EU and EFTA member states. ANEC has already become an associate member of CEN, the European standardisation committee, and participated in the General Assembly of CENELEC, the European standardisation committee for electro-technical products. Through this direct representation at this political level and through direct participation and the co-ordination of national representation at the technical level, ANEC will seek to ensure that consumer interests are adequately addressed by the European standards bodies. ANEC will also work with Consumers International to ensure that consumer interests are addressed at the international level where this directly impacts on European standards projects. As a result of the co-operation agreements that exist between the European standards bodies and their international counterparts, much of the European standardisation work is being carried out within the international standards bodies. In fact, in the case of electro-technical standards, almost 90 per cent of European standards are identical to their international counterparts.

Consumer representatives also have much to contribute in the field of conformity assessment. Consumer organisations can, for example, identify problems with the integrity of conformity assessment schemes through their comparative testing activities and market surveys. Such testing can also help mobilise market forces which can greatly improve the levels of safety to be found in the market place. Examples of this type of testing include the US New Car Assessment Program, NCAP, and the publication of crash test results from the Insurance Institute of Highway Safety, which seeks to drive the safety levels beyond the mandatory minimum standards. At a political level consumer representatives have also participated in the development of such schemes as the new Keymark in Europe, ensuring that consumer concerns surrounding the integrity and the meaning of the mark were addressed in the rules. Next year COPOLCO will continue this dialogue at the international level by holding a joint workshop with CASCO, ISO's conformity assessment policy committee.

Consumers International is also attempting to put pressure on trans-national corporations with the recent launch of their code of conduct for global businesses. CI's charter fills the need for a comprehensive cross-industry code of practice that will set the bounds of ethical behaviour from the consumer perspective. Specifically, the code focuses on four areas: competition, standards, consumer information, and marketing practices. With respect to standards, the charter requires goods produced by trans-national corporations to meet generally accepted international levels, or minimum standards no less stringent than those comparable in the country concerned.

Through the wide-ranging discussion it will facilitate among the different market partners, the OECD conference will undoubtedly help us to understand the problems facing us today and the solutions that can be applied.

Bernard VAUCELLE

It is important to reiterate that the increasing globalisation of trade has had an enormous influence on the development of national, and increasingly, regional and international product safety regulations. The evolution of new technologies has created increasingly numerous and varied innovations, which are in many cases now considered basic needs of our modern life. In this spirit we continue to innovate, to introduce products which are different from their predecessors or from those of competitors, employing technologies of increasing complexity.

Thus we confront products and materials from sources that are no longer confined to the ones with which we are familiar. I want to highlight that this expansion to a global scale has brought a certain anonymity of the producer or of the distributor who puts those products or services into circulation on the market. They can be made at the other side of the world, assembled in another country, and distributed across the rest of the world. In essence, the identity of a manufacturer is no longer transparent for a consumer.

This has compelled regulators at all levels to develop regulations to protect consumers, and consumers to band together to protect their interests. At the same time, an expansion in standardisation has occurred, both by firms interested in establishing an industrial base, and also by regulators, who viewed standardisation as a complementary tool to regulation, especially during the recent move toward deregulation. But a great deal remains to be done in the area of consumer product safety. Today, consumers are better informed and better organised, and can judge and choose the products they want. They can determine characteristics and performance based on increasingly transparent data, both in the area of safety and in other areas such as durability, maintenance, and environmental protection. Certification and standardisation today constitute the tools of a developing policy at the economic, technical and commercial levels which tries to take new data and innovation into account.

The result is a world which is not ideal, not perfect, and not uniform. Countries are at different levels of economic, technological and social development, and we cannot consider our industrialised countries to be the same as African, Latin American or East Asian countries. This might be a problem for those who see the world as a perfect world where there should be one standard, one rule, where goods would circulate without any problem. But the reality is not so perfect: different standards of living, and varied cultural and social values make it difficult to harmonise standards or certification systems.

Standard systems may respond to the expectations of consumers or manufacturers who bear the responsibility for products they introduce on the market. They may aid in opening global markets and decreasing the number of technical barriers or expensive duplicate testing and certifications. But they are neither an easy nor a complete solution, because the underlying economic, social and technical realities are not uniform in the present world.

Today, there are 110 national organisations of standardisation across the world. In the field of voluntary standards, two major organisations co-ordinate international standardisation activity. There are regional levels of standardisation covering more or less all parts of the world, of which the best example today is the European Union. The European Union started on the premise that while Western European countries were at different levels of technological, social and economic development, those levels were close enough for regulation bodies to reach an agreement on general safety aims. That gave birth, in Europe, to what we call the "New Approach" and the adoption of "New Approach Directives." These define, in the framework of the European Union, safety rules in terms of aims to be reached without defining the precise method of achieving those aims, and give public and private market participants the task of finding the definition of harmonised standards at the European level.

At the global level, ISO and IEC together produce 1200 to 1300 standards a year, an enormous production. Throughout the world, there are about 2500 to 3000 working groups for ISO and IEC, including approximately 100 000 engineers, manufacturers, representatives of the public authorities, consumers, experts in the field of research, and lawyers in national delegations working on international standards. Of the over 700 standards a year which are European, 60 per cent come from the international level. So, Europe is involved in harmonisation work on an international basis, and there are agreements between the European organisations and the world organisations so that, when possible, European work is dealt with at the international level.

Is there a way of facilitating trade without increasing technical barriers due to standards? I think we can answer both yes and no. When standards are voluntary, theoretically there are no obstacles.

Manufacturers have a major incentive to adopt voluntary certification: the manufacturer adds value to his product through a signal to the market that the product meets certain requirements, providing the basis for increased consumer confidence. It is therefore important for all parties to clarify the meaning of a certification. Voluntary certification must also be contrasted with third-party certification, which is conducted by an independent organisation which is neither the manufacturer, consumer, nor seller. The most elaborate, which seems to give the greatest levels of confidence and assurance, is a certification which adheres to strictly defined standards, laboratory testing and manufacturing controls. The other kind of voluntary certification is the simple manufacturer's self-declaration. It is conceivable that some consumers may have doubts, in a world of fierce competition, about self-declaration.

I would like to say a few words about the CE mark required in Europe. We cannot associate this mark with a form of certification. The CE mark only means that the product is in compliance with basic safety requirements. It does not take into account the product performance or ensure a permanent control on the product. It is, in essence, a mark which enables public authorities and customs officers to identify circulating products.

I would like to conclude by saying that after having described this imperfect world, there is a strong and important tendency towards harmonisation despite the obstacles. We can suggest that the activity is sometimes insufficient, we can criticise some delays and unharmonised standards, but I am not convinced that if the systems did not exist, it would lead to a world with fewer technical barriers to trade.

We must continue to harmonise without slowing down innovations. Standards must not lead to monoproducts or uniformed products, and rules must not lead to decreased competition. Standardisation mechanisms must be transparent because they are tools which allow the consumer to judge, to make his choice. Without any common language, terminology, testing methods, or systems of reference, I will let you imagine how difficult it would be for the consumer to compare products.

David MILLER

How consumer safety standards and conformity assessment are implemented in countries around the world will have an important impact upon the well-being of my industry. The toy industry could never be considered at the cutting edge from the point of view of the technologies employed. However, we believe we are a cutting edge industry in the sense that we have been global for 25 years, and it is fair to say that the medium-sized and large companies in the toy industry both manufacture and market their products in as many countries as they are permitted to operate.

In the United States, consumers purchase 2 billion toys each year and our marketing information indicates that at any one point in time there are more than 120 000 different stock-keeping units in retail stores. However, only 20 per cent of toy purchases are products made in the United States. We do, however, design, invent, engineer and create the marketing programmes for more than 60 per cent of all toys consumed in the world. Our major companies now sell more products outside the US than they do inside the United States. We believe that most consumer products industries, especially those with high labour content, will have profiles similar to our own. Market research clearly indicates that consumer tastes in economically developed countries or in developing countries are the same.

Obviously, one can not sell beef hamburgers in India nor pork in the Middle East, but people living above the subsistence level with discretionary income and leisure time tend to want the same things. This phenomenon is driven in my opinion by television and the ability of virtually all people to instantaneously see how other people live around the world. You may ask what is the point that I am labouring to make. It is simply that the toy industry, as well as many other industries, are facing a world demand for safe, well-made products sold at fair prices. How easy or how difficult is it to market a product with world-wide demand, and how easy is it to produce that product? Since we are fast approaching Christmas, it is only fair that we play with one of my toys and see if we can answer those questions. Let's look at the production side of my little white friend (a teddy-bear) which is rather simple in appearance.

My friend was made in the Peoples Republic of China. However, all of the components with the exception of polycore thread came from other countries. His beautiful eyes were moulded in Japan and were fixed ultrasonically by a machine made in Korea. The colourful dress was imported from France. The stuffing material of polyester fibre comes from either West Germany or the United States, and the pile fabric was produced in South Korea. All of the components were married in South China. Whose bear is it, though it's mine now? Well, the bear was created in the design rooms of a mid-sized US manufacturer, whose engineers produced the manufacturing and safety specifications for the company's customers in Canada, Mexico, Brazil, the European Union, Japan and the United States. For shipments to the United States, let us look at some of the standards regulations which must be observed. Because some of the bears are sold on a direct basis FOB Hong Kong to four different general merchandise retailers, four different certificates from four different Hong Kong laboratories must be obtained, each certifying that the toy is in compliance with US federal regulations as well as ASTM F-963, the voluntary toy safety standard. Of course, to take advantage of freight rates, the product is shipped for Canada, Brazil and Mexico at the same time.

This means that the labels and handtags on the toy will appear in English, Spanish and French, and products headed for Brazil will require certification from a recognised American or Brazilian laboratory as to compliance with the standard which is partially American and partially European in origin. Parenthetically, illegal copies of this toy -- also made in China -- will be smuggled into Brazil or Paraguay, a country whose economy is based in part upon US$ 10 billion of smuggling a year. But as a result of the MERCOSUR agreement between Argentina, Brazil, Uruguay and Paraguay, this toy can move freely between all four countries.

For the shipments headed toward Japan, the Japanese "ST" mark was placed on the tags and labels to indicate compliance with Japanese toy safety regulations. However, since this toy is intended for children of all ages, including mine, it must meet the formaldehyde testing requirements on infant products.

Another container is headed for an Italian port to be distributed throughout the European Union. It will, of course, have handtags and labels with the appropriate "CE" mark on it, indicating compliance with EN71, the European toy safety standard. The company making this toy has designated its London office as the official site for the "technical file" which establishes the fact that the company uses quality assurance methods and has necessary systems to assure compliance with European toy safety standards.

Now, the quality assurance manager of this American manufacturer went to sleep one night and had a nightmare. What did he dream? First that the US shipment arrived in the port of Seattle and was held up at US customs for an examination of the shipment for safety reasons. There is an agreement between the US Consumer Product Safety Commission and the US customs service to monitor shipments of toys into the US ("Operation Toyland"). This entailed the stripping of a 40 foot container at a cost of close to US$ 2 000 so that the US customs service could randomly select samples of this toy plus several others in the container. The shipment, in a new container, then went to a warehouse in the State of Oregon pending laboratory approval of the samples taken by US customs. The nightmare was not over. The shipment headed for Italy was held in Milan by the customs inspector who requested the technical file for examination upon entry into the European Union. The file was maintained in the English language. When the file arrived several days later, while demurrage charges were being assessed, the customs inspector requested that the file be translated into Italian.

Let me make it clear that I am not criticising the regulatory authorities in any of the countries in which this bear appeared, because they have every right to protect the safety of their own consumers. I am just repeating a scenario which happens every day and which manufacturers are required to accept if they want to do business around the world.

Obviously, there is a cost involved, not only in monetary terms but in terms of time. Moreover, it's clear to me that small companies are precluded from making this product and organisations that try to do it have an awful lot of trouble. They just do not have the resources to absorb the expenses of testing, certification, and procurement.

The conclusions that I will draw from this story are several. First, one could substitute the bear for a television set, an automobile or a sausage and the story line would be the same.

Second, while we speak glibly of world markets and global consumers, it would be inappropriate to conclude that one can freely make and freely buy on the same basis throughout the world. Free and open markets are an ideal and we are still wrestling with how to use existing international institutions or create new ones that will make this possible.

Third, although technology has internationalised communications, knowledge and commerce, we remain within the same state political structures of the last several hundred years, and that is true too in the European Union because all 18 countries are still independent and sovereign in most respects. It seems to me that this is probably the single biggest cause of friction and that is the reason we are meeting today. Global standards and mutual recognition of conformity assessment would go long way toward reducing this friction, while at the same time allowing manufacturers as well as consumers to meet their own needs.

Jürgen NEUN

The world-wide free movement of goods without trade barriers is the wish of every product manufacturer and supplier. The consumer benefits from world-wide free trade through a greater assortment of goods and the increased possibility to select a product suited to his particular needs. This requires above all a sense of confidence in the products being offered. They have to be safe and functional.

Products, like technical requirements, develop nationally, and are linked to the habits of the social environment in which they are used. Through the regionalisation and globalisation of our society, these habits have evolved and new knowledge has been acquired about the potential variety of products in the marketplace. This has led to a transition in product standardisation from the national to the European or global level -- with greater or lesser emphasis, depending on the industry or product group concerned.

The harmonisation of product requirements in state-of-the-art technical regulations is, by itself, insufficient. In order to secure the free movement of goods across borders, it is also necessary to harmonise legislation. The development of a single market within the European Union shows how confidence-building measures can be developed to achieve mutual acceptance of products.

The "New Approach of the European Commission, 1985" toward technical harmonisation and standardisation contains, to that end, certain political prerequisites: These include the issuance of directives on "essential product requirements" for the approximation of national legislation and the fulfilment of these requirements through standardisation. With the goal of achieving the most unified product assessment possible, the "New Approach" was expanded to include a "Global Approach to Certification and Testing."

Depending on product risk, various conformity assessment measures should be established. These range from a Manufacturer's Declaration up to third-party testing and certification, and include the necessary product surveillance procedures or quality control systems. Confidence is an important prerequisite for this system to function. Confidence-building measures for the consumer include proof of competence, and transparency on the part of the manufacturer and the testing laboratory. This translates into a simple formula:

Competence + Transparency = Confidence

The manufacturer encourages consumer confidence by placing value on making products conform to standards, and by making use of a quality control system in the course of production. Testing, certification and surveillance bodies demonstrate their competence by their technical qualifications, and employment of Good Laboratory Practices in line with European Standards Series DIN EN 45000, as well as by their independence and integrity. This standards series, based on ISO guidelines, extensively regulates the criteria for the operation and evaluation of testing laboratories and certification bodies. A product which successfully meets these criteria receives a CE mark as a ticket for the transnational movement of goods.

At first glance, this structural harmonisation procedure is a step forward, but problems may arise from the poor definition of requirement areas and through the overlapping of EU directives. In some cases, the evaluation of a product requires the application of a variety of directives with varying conformity assessment measures. A lack of specificity in the standards for the evaluation and testing of a product leaves manufacturers and testing laboratories latitude to interpret the standards. Whereas, in the set-up of *national* standards, the participating parties -- working from a common technological basis -- have to reduce their interests to a common denominator, in the *global* harmonisation of technical standards, not only the various interests of the participating parties, but various technological, legal, application-specific and customary factors have to be made to agree at a certain level as well. This is a difficult task. The matter is further complicated by the divergent developments of those areas which are regulated by legislation, and those which are not.

To the extent that the manufacturer, in accordance with the prerequisites of EU directives, is not itself responsible for conformity assessment, notified bodies take over this task within those areas regulated by legislation. These bodies have the task of attesting to conformity with directives and legislation, and are completely self-sufficient in issuing their evaluation. In contrast, the unregulated area lacks an enforcement authority. There is considerably greater room in judging the competence of testing and assessment bodies and the evaluation of products.

The attempt to establish a single system for evaluating the competence of testing and certification bodies -- through the accreditation of these bodies and through mutual acceptance of multilateral agreements -- would lead to the erection of a complex and unmonitorable bureaucracy which would be expensive and inflexible, and add no noticeable value to these bodies.

Consensus is indispensable to the acceptance of all measures. The sooner consensus is reached in this process, the easier the process will be. Only standardised requirements that clearly address all relevant aspects of the evaluation process can prevent the possibility of differing interpretations. This possibility would in fact lead to potentially conflicting product assessments, either on the part of the manufacturer, or by the testing and certification bodies. In order to achieve a global marketplace, it is necessary above all to establish international standards. These standards need to be carefully worked out by all interested and affected parties. Since we are all consumers, we all have an interest in the formulation of these standards.

Depending on product risk, standards conformity assessment by a neutral body should be considered. The assessment procedures, including a monitoring function as needed, should also be established in the course of the standardisation in consultation with the affected parties. Conformity of the product can be documented by means of a mark which is granted at the end of the process.

Standards conformity means the comprehensive examination of all the standardised requirements. It will enjoy the highest acceptance because all standardised stipulations are determined by consensus. This should also satisfy consumers' interests and create a basis for confidence. The consumer will choose a product which meets the standards -- that is, one which is safe and functional.

Panel II

CONFORMITY ASSESSMENT SYSTEMS

Chairman

Mr. Nils RINGSTEDT
Vice Chairman - OECD Committee on Consumer Policy
Chairman of the Working Party on Consumer Safety
Deputy Director-General
National Board for Consumer Policies
Sweden

Summary of Remarks

Panellists

Mr. S. Joe BHATIA
Vice President, Follow-Up Services
Underwriters Laboratories Inc.
United States

Mr. Alan BRYDEN
Director General
Laboratoire National d'Essais (LNE)
France

Mr. Daniel PIERRE
Director
Comité Français d'Accréditation (COFRAC)
France

Mr. Charles LUDOLPH
Director
Office of European Community Affairs
Department of Commerce
United States

Mr. David STANGER
Secretary General
European Organisation for Testing and Certification (EOTC)
Belgium

Product certification in its broadest meaning encompasses all types of activities that are designed to build confidence that products, systems and services meet specified standards or criteria. Before discussing other subjects, I would like to briefly summarise some of the major issues of international trade that have certainly had an impact on United States and European counterparts, as well as on other trading partners of United States.

In the beginning of the century, trade was divided into independent individual markets. Because of the strong internal economic and population expansion, there was little need for the US industry to seek markets abroad. Technological advancements and local opportunities allowed industry to focus primarily on domestic markets. The international trading system which emerged after the Second World War changed this US-centred approach. Today we have a global marketplace, which in many industries includes a variety of economically strong nations and trading regions. This recent integration into international markets has also had a significant impact on product certifiers. Being a product certifier myself, I would like to address the issue from that perspective.

In my company, Underwriters Laboratories, 30 years ago only one per cent of our activity came from clients located in 10 countries. Today more than 40 per cent of our activities originate from clients that are based in 90 countries outside the United States. That is how dramatic the shift has been. As major trade barriers such as quotas and import rules are lowered by multilateral trade agreements such as EU, NAFTA and GATT, less significant trade barriers such as conformity assessment standards are emerging as the primary obstacles to trade.

Because of my experience in initiatives to reduce these barriers, I will focus on practical approaches that can be considered in dealing with changes in the trade environment. These include internationalising existing activities, and producing totally new services to accommodate changes in the global marketplace. In the area of international activities, I will present examples to show how certifiers' activities in the United States and key countries have changed or are likely to change in the future.

The basis of conformity assessment programs in any market is specific requirements against which the product must be evaluated. These must be developed in detail through the process of standards harmonisation. National bodies in each country are changing to meet the international demands of today's markets. For example, we at UL are involved in 151 safety standards committees, each of which address a large number of standards categories. We are also actively involved with standardisation activities with Canada, Mexico and in many committees in IEC/ISO.

In all countries standards harmonisation is usually driven by national industry, and is based on their priorities, needs, and the commitment to devote resources to seeking that harmonisation. EU member states are involved in massive standardisation harmonisation via ISO/IEC, CEN, CENELEC, ETSI and other organisations. Japan as well is moving towards a more aggressive harmonisation approach, especially in the quality area. Such efforts will go a long way towards reducing or eliminating duplicative compliance work.

In addition to standards, the certification process is being overhauled to accommodate the requirements of the global market. Certifiers need to continue to respond to the gradual evolution of world-wide product design and production. These days all elements of product and service certification must be delivered throughout most of the world in a timely and cost-effective fashion. Facilitating the certification process would create easier access to foreign markets for manufacturers, no matter where they are based. Without this, many producers have no chance to survive.

Certifiers in the United States and Europe are pursuing bilateral, and in some cases, multilateral agreements in the private arena. This is an opportunity for manufacturers to co-operate with their counterparts in other countries. It is also a confidence-building exercise, and creates methods by which we can validate data developed in local markets and have it accepted in foreign markets. At UL we have established 36 bilateral agreements with our counterparts in different countries. These arrangements help manufacturers sell in Germany, Japan, Korea, Taiwan, Canada, Brazil, and others. Through cross-trading, counterchecks, and right of rejection, we can build confidence, and certifiers can assure that the imported product in a given market complies with the same criteria with which local products must comply, and that it receives similar acceptance in the marketplace. Information relative to standards, codes, laws and requirements can help manufacturers decide how to meet acceptance criteria in foreign countries, and in many cases to decide if it is worthwhile to export in the first place.

The fastest growing export compliance system today is ISO/EN 9 000. These standards are evolving into sub-ISO 9 000 standards very quickly, for example ISO 14000. These demands are driven by government regulations as well as market forces. At UL, approximately 40 per cent of our registration activities involve co-registration which is accepted in both domestic and foreign markets, which enables our clients to reach other markets with certification that is credible and accepted, but accreditation may not always assure market acceptance. In many parts of the world differing requirements, often minimal, create a high threshold that must be crossed before the producer can have his work accepted in a foreign market. Because of the high cost of accreditation, we must make sure that the unnecessary duplicate standards and certification criteria are not applied as a barrier to trade.

Globalisation is a term that is used often these days and has many different meanings. To product certifiers it means continued internationalisation of existing services, as well as new services to meet the change in demand. We must enhance the certification process to satisfy manufacturers' purposes, while at the same time ensuring acceptance by governmental and local authorities, and by retailers, wholesalers and consumers. This must be done not only for the local market, but also for the exporting market. The certifiers of the future will need to possess commitment, experience and tremendous flexibility. Most significantly they must be aware of changes in international markets, and this requires transparency in foreign standards and certification processes.

Alan BRYDEN

I would like to present the point of view of a test and certification operator, and discuss the growing role we will play in the context of free international trade, and in the field of conformity assessment. As an introduction, it is particularly important to note the following developments:

-- generic legislation in product safety has developed in many countries, resulting in general testing obligations for manufacturers and distributors. Specific or sectoral legislation has also been developed based on the notion of essential requirements. These requirements are drafted in general terms rather than in terms specifying very detailed technical criteria;

-- international harmonisation has been the preferred method of avoiding technical trade barriers;

-- there is a tendency to deregulate and to remove from administrations their technical role in conformity assessment of products. This necessitates designating bodies outside the administrations to make conformity assessments, which before were directly carried out by administrations. This development is related both to budgetary issues and to initiatives towards greater liberalisation of trade;

-- new technologies and new priorities, such as environmental protection, which are related to all different types of products, have coincided with the emergence of microprocessors, information technologies, new materials, electromagnetic compatibility phenomenon, etc., making consumer products more complex.

As far as conformity assessment is concerned, considered independently of the legal obligations which result from the generic regulations I mentioned, three factors are pushing us to simplify the process of conformity assessment:

-- international trade, with the GATT agreement and the establishment of the single market in Europe;

-- the reduction of delays between research and development and the marketing of products. For some consumer goods, this cycle has been shortened to a few months;

-- the rapid evolution of technologies, which means that unique product components are being constantly developed.

In Europe and the rest of the world, we are moving towards a regulatory model for product safety compatible with the liberalisation of trade. This model is based on generic legislation that lays down essential requirements, and delegates responsibility for standards development to a consensus process. This process includes industry and consumers who examine the technical details for compliance with essential requirements, limiting the role of administrations to a market monitoring role. Mutual recognition of tests and certificates makes it easier for manufacturers, who now bear the legal responsibility, to do "one-stop testing" and "one-stop certification".

In Europe, we are witnessing the development of accreditation through the EN-45000 standards and parallel works carried out by ISO on codification of different functions related to conformity assessment. These can include accreditation of test laboratories or certification bodies. I believe the term "Fortress Europe" is a misnomer, because we are making a lot of efforts to solve the problems of free trade of goods and reduction of technical barriers. When we compare what we are doing in Europe with other places in the world, which are based on federal systems, I am not sure that the same levels of harmonisation and the same models for simplifying the approach have been reached.

In the conformity assessment sector, we have codified different ways of demonstrating conformity to essential requirements. We have standards that allow us to translate them. Despite this, in Europe we still have difficulty establishing the correspondence between conformity modules and the applicable standards, which are not always clear. Like the ISO, there has been an attempt to create sufficient documentation to clarify areas where correspondence is not yet perfect. Among the different options to ensure conformity assessment of products before they are marketed in Europe, one finds the manufacturers' self-declaration. This is of course something that the manufacturers do at their own risk, and they assume all responsibility for its efficacy.

One of the aspects of the development of codification of conformity assessment has been the development of accreditation. That phenomenon, which began at international level in the last 15 years, has been essentially oriented towards accreditation of testing laboratories. Some years ago, we saw accreditation developing for certifying bodies, products and systems of quality assurance. Now, accreditation for inspection bodies is developing, including accreditation of environmental standards and inspection bodies. An international acceptance of the results of tests and certificates through agreements on accreditation bodies should simplify mutual recognition.

There is still one aspect of accreditation which must be clarified, and that is the relationship between accreditation and services certification or quality systems certification. There has been some mixing of categories which leads to confusion and must be rectified.

In conclusion, I believe that the following points are the keys to success in order to reconcile potential conflicts between international trade with consumer safety. International trade should not be improved to the detriment of product safety. Should that be the case, we would have missed our goal.

First, there should be more international co-operation on standards development. One must not forget that standardisation is not only a means to facilitate international trade but also a means to determine essential scientific and technical requirements for products and for safety.

The second key to success is more clarity in standards definition. Standards which are not accurate about the methods to follow result in misinterpretation at laboratories and certifying bodies levels. That is definitely not the way towards true harmonisation and technical conformity.

The third key to success is organising the role in the interpretation of standards which standardisation committees should play. This especially concerns the jurisprudence of the standards interpretation. We are facing the problem of varying interpretations of standards. Because of deregulation, the understanding of the law is based on the interpretation of the underlying standard, which makes this a particularly crucial area.

The fourth key is having accreditation done according to performance standards rather than design standards.

The final key is mutual recognition, either between accreditation bodies or at the state level, as is presently negotiated between the European Union and third countries. Those agreements have to be based on mutual technical confidence and not exclusively on political or commercial considerations. In this way we can best ensure safe products and functioning global markets.

Daniel PIERRE

In 1993, France decided to introduce a single and comprehensive accreditation system which would allow it to demonstrate that French test and calibration laboratories and certification organisations complied with the EN 45000 series of standards and the guidelines established within the broader framework of the ISO. This system of accreditation was to be administered by a new body, COFRAC (Comité Française d'Accréditation), which was established on 29 April 1994.

COFRAC assumed the accreditation activities previously undertaken by the RNE (National Testing Network) for testing and analytical laboratories, and by BNM-FRETAC (National Metrology Office) for standards-testing laboratories. COFRAC embarked upon developing accreditation in areas which had not previously been covered in France, such as the accreditation of certification bodies for products and quality systems for firms and personnel, and of environmental auditors in compliance with the European Union's "eco-audit" regulations. To best accomplish this mission, it was decided that COFRAC would comply with both existing European and international standards (EN 45003 and ISO/IEC Guide 58), and proposed future standards (EN 45010 and ISO/CASCO Guide 226).

COFRAC is a non profit-making association registered under the Act of 1 July 1901. Its members are divided into four sections:

-- laboratories and bodies which are already accredited or which have applied for accreditation;

-- manufacturer's associations which use the services of the laboratories or bodies in the above section;

-- end users, consumer groups and public procurement officials; and

-- public authorities.

In addition, suitably qualified persons may become associate members. It is not, of course, necessary to be a member to apply for accreditation.

COFRAC receives its funding from membership dues; fees charged for processing, issuing and monitoring accreditation; and government subsidies, which will be reduced after the current initial period. It has a Board of Administration consisting of 22 members representing the four sections referred to above. To ensure that the Board's decisions are impartial, no single section is allowed to have a majority voting position. COFRAC is divided into eight accreditation sections, each consisting of approximately 20 members according to the same scheme as the Board of Administration:

COFRAC is very much involved in the work being undertaken at the European and international level by the following associations of accreditation bodies:

-- EAC, European Accreditation of Certification;
-- EAL, European Co-operation for Accreditation of Laboratories;
-- IAF, International Accreditation Forum;
-- ILAC, International Laboratory Accreditation Conference.

COFRAC is a member of the EAL multilateral mutual recognition agreement on product and standards testing, and also intends to sign the EAC agreement as soon as possible. It actively participates in comparative surveys of laboratories. Thus COFRAC, whose work involves both voluntary and mandatory standards, is in a position to perform the task it has been assigned, namely to help foster the climate of confidence needed to avoid the unnecessary proliferation of testing, auditing and certification activities.

Charles M. LUDOLPH

For more than a decade, international trade has expanded faster than most of our domestic economies. For most manufacturers, international trade is the last and only sure growth market. Tariffs have virtually disappeared but standards loom as barriers to trade. In 1993 almost half of total US exports to the world required a product certification. In addition, it is becoming commonplace that almost no one in another market trusts what a foreign manufacturer does anymore, and requirements for formal conformity assessment are multiplying. In the old days, even five years ago, a US manufacturer could comply with a domestic requirement -- obtain a UL listing, an FAA air-worthiness certification, an EPA or FDA certification for a drug or chemical, and they could go to virtually any foreign market, present the certificate issued domestically for sale in the United States, and almost any third country market would accept that certificate. They would say, "Fine. If it's good enough for the United States, it's good enough for us."

Today that's not true. I had the pleasure, recently, of sharing a program with the Chief Regulatory Engineer for the Dell Computer Company. Dell introduces 180 new products a year which have an average product life of eight months. Almost half of Dell's sales are international. In 1991, the Dell regulatory compliance department was required to get five regulatory approvals to sell around the world: something for local US electrical sales, a certification from a local US electrical lab, a US FCC approval, a German VDE approval and a Canadian CSA approval; five approvals for 180 products, and they were in business world-wide.

But things have changed enormously. In 1996, Dell projects that they will have to get 26 approvals around the world for these 180 products. In Europe alone, instead of getting two approvals and using Germany as the basis for the approvals, the Chief Regulatory Engineer also has to get the CE mark, SEMKO, NEMKO, and he expects that he will have to get a mark for Slovakia and also a mark for the Ukraine.

Mexico now has a mark. Japan now doesn't require marks but it does require certification to European standards. Several ergonomic standards are now being required by Japan, and the basis for these are EN standards.

Now Dell is faced with an unimaginable bill for redundant certifications that could well be accelerated and reduced by a well-built international accreditation system. The absence of an accreditation system -- of course the absence of regulators to co-operate and harmonise, the absence of harmonised standards, but even more importantly, the absence of a regulator's recognition that a test certificate, or a process registration certificate, from a single entity accredited internationally as acceptable in world markets -- presents them with a high-cost bill.

Not everybody in this room is selling in 85 markets and introduces 180 products per year. Not everybody is faced with that kind of challenge today, but it is certain that they will be faced with the challenge of international trade as manufacturers and regulators in the near future. Every day more people are getting a larger international bill for regulatory acceptance than they ever have before. This is an unacceptable situation. You can no longer use only a US-based or a European-based certificate in international trade. The US international trade has doubled in the last seven years, from about five per cent to ten per cent of GDP, but the cost of obtaining market access is skyrocketing under pressures to formalise national conformity assessment requirements.

It is very hard to convince a US businessperson or regulator, even today, that foreigners want a new formal and third party based conformity assessment system because today in the United States our system is held together by consumer and workplace product liability. Why do people get along building safe products in the United States without somebody overseeing them? Why does manufacturer self-certification work in the United States? Why don't we have higher accident statistics, and more deaths than anybody else? The glue that holds us together is the manufacturers' fear of product liability and other torts. Many other important OECD countries have a similar high requirement for liability and insurance systems, such as the German workers' compensation requirements covering products used in the work place. As long as these insurance-based requirements are based on national conformity assessment, costs will remain prohibitively high for international trade.

Today all involved in the system recognise the problem of redundant and unnecessary conformity assessment requirements and their effect on trade and consumer costs, with very little incremental consumer protection gained. Today regulators, insurance companies, and test bodies and standardisers have developed a host of high-cost approaches that the market cannot support to address the issues. Extensive webs of bilateral MOUs or MRAs have been initiated as well as endless programs of global harmonisation initiatives over regulatory practices. International accreditation, sometimes called "designation" or "listing programmes," have been established. All have the view of overcoming the limits of national requirements, but unfortunately provide no near term prospect of lowering costs.

While these efforts mentioned above should not be ignored for their potential, there has been relatively little discussion on their potential for success. MRAs, for example, were invented to facilitate trade within the European Union and associated countries based on identical product safety standards. There is very little regulatory evidence that this system can be applied to areas where product standards have not been harmonised, and this issue represents the chief obstacle to completion of two years of negotiation. Similarly, private sector based systems, with their inherent conflicts of interest and antitrust implications, need to be examined to determine if they reduce transaction costs in proportion to their protection of consumers interests. Since all these initiatives -- MRAs, harmonisation, international standardisation -- require an enormous amount of resources, governments and manufacturers need to know there is a payoff.

Such analysis of the costs and benefits of these diverse initiatives to internationalise conformity assessment needs to be undertaken, and has yet to be convincingly addressed. One region pursues bilateral MRAs, a global regulatory community pursues international harmonisation, another product sector looks at defining international equivalence. There is an approach to conformity assessment for every sector traded in the world, and there is no commitment of any of the users to rely on these international systems for their merits. Manufacturers and consumers alike pay the price for the divergences and redundancies.

A broader range of interested parties, e.g. regulators and insurance companies, needs to be brought into the development of international requirements for conformity assessment. National insurance systems, particularly those with ties to government safety laws, generally do not accept foreign standards or manufacturers' certifications without some form of third party intervention. We need a system where insurers recognise the equivalence of third party evaluations.

There is also a profusion of unnecessary conformity assessment standards that need to be addressed either by formalisation or harmonisation. OECD GLPS are almost identical to ISO CASCO Guides on lab performance, but are not deemed equivalent by regulators. Similarly, national GMPs are not deemed equivalent to ISO 9000. Many governments and insurance companies maintain informal listing programs of manufacturers, labs and certifiers which reflect little or no international consensus. Governments, regulators and private sector certification systems should be invited to formalise these systems and base them on objective criteria -- perhaps even on international objective criteria.

There is a growing demand for reducing the transaction costs of conformity assessment. National regulators cannot afford to police all borders and all products to the safety standards that the marketplace requires. There are now too many potential suppliers to any single market. As health care costs come under pressure and containment initiatives grow, tort insurance systems will be under new pressure to perform. National private and public insurance systems and manufacturers will be required to respond to international demands.

David STANGER

In 1993 the European Organisation for Testing and Certification (EOTC) was incorporated under Belgian Law with a mandate to be the focal point for conformity assessment issues in Europe. In 1994 the General Assembly of EOTC adopted the first Five Year Business Plan. The main objective of EOTC is to contribute to the harmonious development of quality-oriented activities in Europe (testing, certification, accreditation, etc.) by constituting a focal point for all parties in these areas of activities.

Within the latest edition of our Business Plan we have drawn up a challenging business development policy. The policy utilises members expertise whenever available. In collaboration with all our national, European, and associate members. EOTC is now ready to do business with our Members and five Councillors (CEC, EFTA, CEN, CENELEC and ETSI) to improve the European quality image and confidence in harmonised testing and certification services. We will utilise, to full effect, the new five year (1995/1999) framework contracts signed with the Commission and EFTA and continue to develop meaningful working arrangements with the European Standards Bodies.

The fora of our Sectoral Committees and their associated Agreement Groups bring together the customer and supplier along with all relevant public and private sector interests and gives opportunity to debate and resolve issues in an environment below the threshold of competitiveness. The successful application of the principle of our Sectoral Committee will provide the participants the opportunity to propose to the regulator a policy for self-regulation within their sector of the European marketplace.

Fora or meetings organised by our Sectoral Committees (ECITC, ELSECOM, ESCIF, EWSC) or by the EOTC Secretariat on issues including the proposed CEN/CENELEC 'Keymark', development of a Handbook for the Telecommunications Terminal Equipment Directive, the accreditation process, and the Third Country MRA negotiations, have enhanced the process of awareness and harmonisation of the testing and certification services to the benefit of industry and their client base in Europe and beyond.

EOTC actively reinforces the work of all our European Members to strengthen and increase confidence in their testing and certification services (EUROLAB, EQS, IIOC, CEOC) and the emerging European accreditation multilateral agreements developed by EAC and EAL. All our Members have substantive programmes to develop and harmonise many aspects of testing and certification.

Our development plan supports the Community eco-management and audit scheme, invites co-operation with central European countries, encourages information exchanges with third countries and seeks to increase the involvement of our European industry base to gain added value from testing and certification services by working within the EOTC structure. By the end of this year our Testing Inspection Calibration and Quality Assurance database (TICQA) containing information on some 2 000 European testing and certification enterprises and our technical library on quality topics will be open for business.

EOTC, as a focal point for conformity assessment:

-- encourages and promotes development of European harmonised certification systems and mutual recognition agreements;

-- provides, through participation in EOTC, all parties with the basis of confidence in test results and certificates issued by Agreement Groups recognised by EOTC, then reducing the need for repeat testing;

-- offers project co-ordination of pre-standardisation work, through the ASSIST programme, to complement or service CEC/EFTA programmes;

-- will assist and complement the European standardisation process in the field of conformity assessment;

-- offers an infrastructure for co-operation between Notified Bodies;

-- disseminates information on European testing and certification services.

Working together, below the threshold of competitiveness, ensures efficient and cost-effective relations between European associations and organisations, public and private, interested in facilitating the trade of safe and quality-oriented products and services.

Panel III

GAINING ACCESS TO THE GLOBAL MARKETPLACE

Chairman

Mr. Naohiro YASHIRO
Member of the Social Policy Council
Japan

Summary of Remarks

Panellists

Mr Hendrik ABMA
Foreign Trade Association
Germany

Mr. J.G. GADDES
Director General
Federation of British Electrotechnical and Allied Manufacturers' Association (BEAMA)
United Kingdom

Mr. Michel MALNOY
Delegate General
Groupement interprofessionnel des fabricants d'appareils d'équipement ménager (GIFAM)
France

Dr. Wim ROGMANS
Secretary General
European Consumer Safety Association (ECOSA)
Netherlands

Hendrik ABMA

The Foreign Trade Association (FTA) represents the interests of the European import retail trade. It fights for free world trade guided by the principles of an international division of labour. The FTA observes that the European Commission as well as the EU member states, above all Germany, increasingly have the tendency to lay down heightened safety requirements for products which are sold on the European market. In the intention of the GATT, such legal product requirements can *de jure* not be considered non-tariff trade barriers as long as they also apply for domestic products and, as such, they cannot be considered discriminatory measures. Nevertheless, in practice, they often have a protectionist impact. I would like to explain this with a concrete example.

In July 1994, the Law on Foodstuffs and Utility Goods ("LMBG") came into effect in Germany. This law prohibits the production, import and introduction into circulation of certain azo-dyes in materials that may cause cancer. The materials affected by the law are not only materials such as textile and clothing products, but also bracelets and frames for glasses. Azo-dyes that can form amines upon division are also prohibited. Therefore, in Germany, it is prohibited to use these dyes for the colouring of the afore-mentioned materials. Other EU member states do not have a similar ban.

In many of the textile exporting countries, this regulation has caused a great disturbance on the governmental as well as industrial level. Foreign exporters insist that there is not sufficient proof of the alleged physical danger of the forbidden dyes. They fear that in the future the relevant legal requirements and regulations will constantly change, thus necessitating frequent new adjustments. Others are opposed to the new requirements because they consider them to be hidden protectionist measures which serve the sale of more expensive German textiles and clothing rather than the protection of health. This ban confronts foreign suppliers with serious application problems, caused by the fact that the rules for an effective implementation of the regulation are not sufficiently clear and precise. Moreover, the exporting countries were not given a sufficient transitional period.

The main problem is that so far there is neither a mutually accepted testing method nor sufficient testing capacities to establish the existence of the harmful amines. In numerous supplier countries, such as India or certain Latin American countries, these tests are at present almost impracticable. As a rule, these countries do not have the same technological standards or the procurement logistics for costly testing systems and materials used in Europe. The poorer developing countries are faced with the problem that for the lack of foreign exchange currency they cannot easily procure substitute testing abroad. Thus, high safety requirements for products also have an impact on development policy.

The information on the new requirements must very often be passed on by importers to foreign suppliers. Many exporters also expect that importers will provide them with the testing method and the technological equipment to satisfy new compliance requirements. Furthermore, it should be mentioned that a mere piece of information from foreign suppliers -- which in many cases are not the manufacturers -- does not suffice to strictly satisfy these requirements. In addition to contractual conformity declarations by each supplier, further controls and safeguards are required by each importer.

The difficulty for manufacturers and suppliers from abroad as well as for the importers is that these requirements, which consist of a complicated network of bans, regulations and evaluation standards, are unmethodical. Moreover, these requirements are subject to rapid changes because there are constantly new findings on sources of danger, levels of harmful concentration, or the injury potential of substances. Differing standards within the European Union as well as among other industrial countries constitute an additional obstacle. The procurement of information is aggravated by the lack of a complete compilation of safety requirements and product standards, as well as by the lack of a central authority on a national or international level which gathers this knowledge and places it at the disposal of the exporting countries.

In order to avoid safety requirements becoming trade barriers, importing as well as exporting countries should comply with the following conditions:

--   requirements must be transparent, i.e. on the one hand, their necessity must be justified, and, on the other hand, exporting countries must receive timely information about the introduction of a new standard which is relevant for export;

--   trade fairs can be used to convey information to firms from exporting countries;

--   exporting countries must be granted an appropriate transitional period for adaptation;

--   the knowledge and technology transfer which is required for the adaptation or re-organisation should be backed by resources which are motivated by trade development policy (such as information programmes and industry co-operation in the field of consumer protection);

--   export products must have access to customary private or national labels insofar as they comply with their criteria. This ensures that otherwise safe and compliant foreign products are not subject to consumer discrimination in favour of labelled products;

--   in order to enable individual exporters in developing countries to fulfil the growing international quality standards, "export monitoring institutions" could be created which assume the guarantee for the quality of the export products vis-à-vis international customers, and which at the same time impose the necessary quality standards upon national producers. Moreover, they could monitor that these quality standards are being observed.

Higher product safety requirements gain constantly in importance as market access criteria, and require a great deal of adaptation from producers in Europe and abroad. Since Europe is an important market outlet for developing countries, these new safety requirements increasingly affect exporters in developing countries. If conflicting product safety issues can be addressed in the way described above, international trade can become a mechanism to enhance global consumer protection.

Gordon GADDES

Modern industrial society is dependent on materials, components, sub-assemblies, products and systems which are manufactured on the basis of standards -- an important component of which is technical specifications.

Measurements are included in these specifications, the precision and the repeatability of which are basic to performance. When selecting products, it is important to have confidence that the product conforms to its technical design specifications. Such confidence is generated by testing the product and/or assessing the capability of a factory to manufacture and supply it in continuing compliance with the specification.

These actions are supported by conformity assessment evidence such as certification marks, certificates, test reports, inspection reports and quality assessment reports. These, in turn, support the identity and the image created by the supplier of the product. They are a basis for marketing, purchasing and servicing the product, as well as possibly supporting litigation and remedies in the face of unsatisfactory performance. In certain cases, the product assessment is so important, for example to user safety, that evidence of compliance with standards is mandatory. Accordingly, each modern nation has its own system of technical requirements, but these requirements constitute technical barriers to trade.

The issue of technical barriers to trade is complex. A barrier to one company, industry or country may provide advantages to another, at least in the medium term. All efforts to remove barriers to trade meet resistance from those who feel threatened. This explains the halting and uneven approach to removing such barriers. Results are not achieved by dictate, but by negotiation which involves a search for consensus and consent.

A single process of conformity assessment saves time and money, supports larger scale production and economies of scale, and helps manufacturers who want to establish confidence in their products in a large, continental market. It simplifies purchasing, thus reducing costs for large industrial companies. In addition to one single global assessment, there are also possibilities for regional solutions to handle evidence of compliance.

At this stage let us stand back a little, and just remind ourselves of what different interests want from the economic process: the consumer and the business user want value for money from a product or system which gives satisfaction in use for the anticipated life span; the regulator wants as few problems as possible in the course of consumption by a satisfied population; and a very specialist interest group, the conformity assessment community, wants to fulfil a role and to maintain or develop their profession and business. This community includes certification bodies, test houses and laboratories, inspectorates and specialised groups of engineers. Even management consultants and accountants can get into the act, an act which is ever-widening. A systems approach was explained to me recently in which the different methods of audit for a company, in relation to the functions of management and production, would be harmonised into a total system to cover financial audit, quality assurance, environmental audit, and occupational safety and health audit.

Where is the manufacturer in all of this? Well, he helps to fuel the system. He wants materials, components and sub-assemblies delivered on time to the standards and quality specified, and he requires assurance of compliance to his purchasing specifications. He also establishes the evidence of compliance necessary or desirable for marketing his product. This is the stage when he feels vulnerable, and about which he is sensitive.

To resort to a third party for evidence of compliance involves costs. A very tight system may involve type approval of products, systematic testing of samples, pre-licensing inspection visits and routine inspection visits, and certification administration costs. Extension of the system to embrace quality management standards adds to costs. Additionally, there are the costs of certification, and reference to the national measurement base. If the manufacturer has to face charges for these activities plus all his related internal costs, he sees a measurable and significant part of total costs associated with evidence of compliance. If this were to give him market entry, ensure unchallenged profitable market

70

position, and provide stability for his future planning he would see this all to be cheap at the price. There are many examples of great national schemes which manufacturers have been happy to support because of marketing imperatives.

However, the commercial environment has changed with the deeper development of European, indeed global supply systems. Now increasingly the manufacturer has to consider what process of conformity assessment is additionally needed for foreign markets. He is critically interested in the systems for conformity assessment which his foreign competitors face. Are they easy, cheaper, faster? He is aware that conformity assessments differ in nature from country to country, especially in cost, time required, and rigour.

One of my members found that he could get a test report, with a promise of a quicker testing turnaround, for £ 1 000 from a continental test house, when the cost from a UK test house was £ 8 000. Perhaps, the UK test house, which incidentally has a great reputation, would produce a "Rolls Royce test report" acceptable throughout much of the world. However, an equal acceptability of the lower-price report, in Western Europe for example, could lead my member to put the work abroad.

It is in these contexts, therefore, that the European Economic Communities, working with the then six EFTA countries, have been encouraging the mutual acceptance of conformity assessment to help to establish a barrier-free regional market. As you know, a range of Directives, Regulations, Standards and other harmonisation documents is being created in Europe.

Agreement upon a common set of technical specifications in the form of European standards is the first step towards the removal of technical barriers to trade within the Community. Another equally important step is mutual recognition of the procedures used to assess the conformity of a product to a standard. Testing and certification procedures are used to check that a product or process complies either with voluntary standards or with statutory regulations. If successfully passed, they result in the issue of certificates of conformity and of the licence to affix a mark.

A typical problem resides in the non-recognition by one EU country of another's certification process. Such a non-recognition is mostly based on special testing arrangements applied in the different countries, depending on the specific test facilities that are used, and leads to additional testing or even to an absolute market entry barrier. Such barriers to trade not only mean additional certification and testing costs to the manufacturing industry. They also tend to force manufacturers to produce tailor-made products for each of the national markets in which they want to sell their products. This market fragmentation means a competitive disadvantage for European industry, especially in relation to competition with the United States and Japan. It implies also higher costs, which at the end of the day are to be borne by the customers.

During the last 25 years, in Western Europe, there have been examples of agreements between national economic partners to accept each other's certificates, test and inspection reports. However, these remain limited in product coverage, and there has not been an overall framework to facilitate growth of mutual acceptance for a continental market until the recent European Union Global Approach to Testing and Certification and the establishment of the European Organisation for Testing and Certification.

Then of course there is the question of conformity assessment arrangements in third countries, including well-developed industrial economies and rapidly developing economies. This represents a further complication and a further need for the introduction of mutual acceptance arrangements on both a bilateral and multilateral basis.

In all of the above I am quoting from the Fourth Simons Lecture, *European Signposts for Conformity Assessment,* which I gave at the Royal Institution in London on 25 November 1993. It is also relevant to quote from the recent ORGALIME statement on Conformity Assessment dated 5 October 1995. ORGALIME represents some 50 000 manufacturing companies in the mechanical, electrical, electronic and metal articles industries in 16 countries, members of the EU, EEA and EFTA, and is vitally concerned to see an efficient conformity assessment system established across Europe, and indeed, in third countries. ORGALIME states that conformity assessment, in terms of its purposes, its complex patterns, its development and rationalisation, is of vital interest to manufacturers. They have to pay for the process, and the additional costs affect their final prices; this is particularly a problem when short runs of products are involved with limited time to market. Increasing world competition and market-impelled design changes give the manufacturer a reduced period to recoup costs and attain profit.

Resort to third party bodies for certification takes time and money. Dependence on certification bodies and/or test houses for approval, for turnaround deadlines, for pricing efficiency, and for professional integrity, can make manufacturers feel vulnerable, and this explains sensitivities to policies which seem to increase the potential for third party involvement. ORGALIME considers conformity assessment a sensitive, costly, and time consuming activity which must be judged in the context of world-wide competition and decreasing life cycles of products.

The key conclusions of ORGALIME confirm the need for a limitation of third party certification, a limitation of the reference in national regulations to third party certification, and the need for the establishment of mutual recognition arrangements within the European Union (a model for which are nine mutual acceptance arrangements in CENELEC) and, where commercially feasible, between the European Union and third countries.

Michel MALNOY

The microwave oven was, according to the standard product definition, "designed to warm and/or cook food with electromagnetic energy." This cooking process emerged in Holland not long after the Second World War. Its industrial development occurred successively in the United States, Japan, Europe, Korea, China and in various other countries. From an economic perspective, the product falls into the category of electronic devices available to the general public. Prices of microwave ovens are falling: from 1985 to 1994, prices in Europe fell by 50 per cent. This is explained by the fact that the manufacturing of the product has been "de-localised." Ovens are sold for the most part under specific widely-recognised industrial marks, although "non-brands" or distribution brands are increasingly emerging.

The microwave oven market is truly a global market, and ovens supplied are practically identical in all of the countries on the planet. Production is extremely concentrated; it consists of approximately 12 major manufacturers around the world, plus companies without industrial "pedigree" created *ex nihilo*, primarily in the People's Republic of China, which supply ovens that are often rather primitive at inexplicably low prices. These practices led European manufacturers to file an antidumping complaint with the European Commission, and American manufacturers are currently studying the same possibility.

In such a context, safety standards and qualification certificates are very important for microwave ovens. This importance, in its international aspects, is nevertheless limited to countries that are open to imports, not only *de jure*, but also *de facto*. What would be the purpose of uniform international standards if certain countries, for various reasons, remained closed to foreign products? Standards have two purposes:

-- to ensure the safety of consumers; and

-- to ensure by their international or harmonised character that they will not hinder the free circulation of products, an important factor for competition and economic progress.

Third-party certification and the fixing of quality marks on products should not be disregarded. It should be mentioned that, to the extent that the quality mark only covers product safety, the safety requirement affecting all products offered for sale takes away from that mark its elitist and thus promotional nature, and may not induce the consumer to choose one product over another. The recognition of quality marks and qualification certificates varies according to the country. In France, only about half of consumers say, generally, that a standards mark constitutes a buying criterion.

The necessity for safety is the same in all countries. Nothing in this respect can justify normative, regulatory or supra-regulatory differences that are observed all too often. This evidence and the concern for ensuring free circulation of products militate entirely in favour of global standardisation. If the content of an international safety standard is not found to be satisfactory, it must be discussed. But it cannot be corrected by the adoption of national deviations. Qualification certificates or "quality seals" present both advantages and disadvantages. If a quality seal exists, it seems desirable, for economic reasons, that to the widest extent, self-certification by industry is preferred to third-party certification. This position obviously does not prevent subsequent controls or the imposition of severe sanctions on manufacturers that place a quality seal on the products when the product does not even satisfy basic safety requirements. This also applies to voluntary qualification certificates.

It is obvious that products should be required to bear qualification certificates. But such provisions more often than not originate from a concern to protect domestic markets rather than to protect consumers. The CE mark, which is progressively being implemented in Europe, constitutes a satisfactory formula, provided that misleading advertisements are severely punished. Agreements of the CO or CCA type authorising national qualification certificates on the basis of tests conducted in a third country present huge advantages, but it is obvious that manufacturers prefer that qualification certificates have an international scope. Serious discussions on these topics are currently being undertaken in Europe.

At a meeting in Durban in November 1995, the President of the IEC said: "The world-wide acceptance of a product tested once, with one single certificate and, if necessary, one single mark is the ultimate objective of the IEC in terms of conformity assessment." Industry leaders agree with this objective.

A role for public authorities

Given these greater concerns about safety issues, one may still question whether society should resort to a strong public authority role (regulating and controlling these risks) instead of relying on the private parties' capabilities to control a proper market functioning.

Consumer product safety should recognise a particular area of public interest if markets prove to be unable to generate effective systems and structures for ensuring safety, consistently and systematically. This inability of private partners to generate systems may be due to their inclination to:

-- monitor only a limited part of the consumer market, which restricts their ability to oversee all relevant modes of application, product offers etc., and to build up a core information and expertise system for setting effective standards and requirements;

-- focus on design features instead of analysing the relevant risks and hazards involved and establishing common standards for addressing these hazards, which are applicable to various product categories;

-- secure information that is relevant for reaching sound standards and regulation, out of fear of losing competitive advantage by providing product information to third parties;

-- emphasise specific interests in product promotion at the cost of providing objective and impartial information to consumers with respect to the risks involved; and

-- not achieve a co-ordinated management of quality control systems that is obeyed by all private parties involved.

Although it is a fallacy to argue that it pays for manufacturers to profitably sell sub-standard products to consumers, as a whole, business is not able to effectively, efficiently and comprehensively control risks related to consumer products. The experiences in the Anglo-Saxon countries have shown that liability regulations alone are insufficient in controlling product safety, and that for effective control an additional set of preventative regulations and monitoring systems are needed. As consumers are unable to assess today's product risks and risks in the home environment due to increased product complexity and invisibility of risks involved, there is an evident need for public protection by authorities.

Tasks to be fulfilled by public authorities

The general task for public authorities should be to promote the improvement of safety for consumers and to protect them from unreasonable risks of injuries associated with consumer products in daily life. The authorities should monitor and evaluate the technical, scientific and economic information required in the field of safety for consumers. Basically these tasks include:

-- management of technical and scientific information necessary for the formulation and evaluation of measures envisaged in this field;

-- promotion of exchange of information on accident reports, studies and investigations and its dissemination to all parties concerned;

-- analysis of relevant statistics on product-related injuries and fatalities, and the dissemination to all parties concerned;

-- advancement of appropriate safety standards and rulemaking, addressing the risks of injury identified through the available statistics and studies;

-- monitoring of the application of regulatory measures and of available technical knowledge with regard to safety of products and features in the home environment and the co-ordination of enforcement intelligence in this field;

-- promotion of safety information programmes and campaigns, targeting at consumers (risk groups) and business as well;

-- acting as a resource centre of expertise and knowledge on consumer safety matters and related fields of expertise;

-- promotion of training courses and permanent education of relevant professionals involved, and liaison with relevant disciplines and academic schools.

Central agency

It is important that there be one agency charged with promoting the safety interests related to products and home environment, which can:

(a) make transparent the work of all relevant governmental and non-governmental bodies;

(b) prevent wasteful duplication of efforts;

(c) identify areas of need not yet covered by authorities and private parties;

(d) seek to ensure the commitment and involvement of all relevant bodies and parties involved in implementing consumer safety programmes.

This should not impede local authorities involvement in consumer safety matters. The general trend is to decentralise public authorities' responsibilities and to promote the commitment of lower level public supervision. However the need remains unchanged for supervision and co-ordination of these tasks at the central level, and having an effective infrastructure for executing these responsibilities.

Panel IV

CONFORMITY ASSESSMENT - MUTUAL RECOGNITION AGREEMENTS

Chairman

Mr. Allan ASHER
Chairman - OECD Committee on Consumer Policy
Deputy Chairman
Competition and Consumer Commission,
Australia

Summary of Remarks

Panellists

Mr. Jacques BLANC
Consultant
International Organisation for Standardisation (ISO)
Switzerland

Mr. John A. CLARKE
Directorate General for External Relations
European Commission
Belgium

Mr. Lars ETTARP
Director-General
Swedish Board for Accreditation and Conformity Assessment (SWEDAC)
Sweden

Mr. J. REPUSSARD
Secretary General
Comité européen de normalisation (CEN)
Switzerland

Ms. Vivien LIU
Economic Affairs Officer
Trade and Environment Division
World Trade Organisation (WTO)
Switzerland

A key word that has recurred in the presentations and discussions so far has been the word *confidence*. Mutual recognition implies mutual confidence, and this cannot be forced from the top. It must be spread by normal market forces and be intimately linked with industrial and trade processes. This means that mutual recognition can only result from the voluntary efforts of all circles concerned, and must be based on agreed criteria. If the benefits of mutual recognition are expected to extend effectively across borders, the best method is to use established international criteria. This is where the International Organisation for Standardisation and International Electrotechnical Commission (ISO/IEC) international standardisation system enters into play.

The ISO/IEC system, with its consensus machinery, its network of standardising bodies, and the individual contributions of thousands of experts world-wide, plays a double role in this context. Its primary role is to channel these voluntary efforts to produce consumer product safety standards that are recognised and applied world-wide, either directly or by integration into regional and national standards. It has already been mentioned that the European standard EN 29000, quoted in several papers, is now designated EN ISO 9000, in line with the new CEN policy to explicitly reflect when a European standard has been assumed unchanged from an ISO international standard. Let us hope that their sister organisation CENELEC will soon adopt the same rule. This would permit even non-informed users to immediately understand that, to take an example quoted in the OECD study distributed at this conference, the European standard EN 60335-2-25 for the safety of microwave ovens, is in fact the international standard IEC 335-2-25.

In its secondary role, and this relates directly to our present topic, the ISO/IEC system produces guidance documents for the assessment of conformity with standards, thus providing the internationally agreed criteria needed to pave the way to mutual recognition across borders.

The standards and standard-like documents issued by ISO and IEC are not formulated by just a few people in Geneva. They are the results of voluntary, concerted efforts and consultation of all parties concerned: producers, users, industry/trade groups, governmental agencies, professional societies, academic circles, organised consumers, etc., which are the prime movers, and at the same time the beneficiaries of ISO/IEC work.

This co-ordinated input of thousands of individuals or groups world-wide is supported by a small but efficient, non-bureaucratic machinery. It results in international standards or standard-like documents, which can be adopted unchanged as national and regional standards. Most of those relevant to this conference have been quoted in the comprehensive study conducted by the OECD Committee and in speakers' presentations, either directly or by reference to the corresponding European standards. In addition, many other international bodies are producing standards, such as ITU (and ETSI) in the telecommunication field, WHO, and the joint FAO/WHO Codex Alimentarius Committee.

Reference has been made at this conference to the work of two of the ISO/IEC policy committees, namely ISO/CASCO for conformity assessment and ISO/COPOLCO for consumer affairs.

International standardisation is indeed a dynamic, continuous improvement process, as it evolves in the real world. I gave the example yesterday of the "it's for real" effect which may lead sometimes to the re-questioning of documents prepared with a strong input from all parts of the world (notably from North America, Asia, Australasia and Europe) and already approved internationally, such as ISO/IEC Guide 25 on the competence of laboratories, before the internationally agreed documents are taken over as national standards or regional standards by those who prepared them (e.g. EN 45001 in the case of ISO/IEC Guide 25). There is no doubt that the present conference and the work of the OECD Committee on Consumer Policy may help to convince all those concerned of the advisability to work "for real" in the preparation of valid international documents which they can then implement directly.

In reference to these ISO/IEC standards or guidelines on conformity assessment, I should mention that ISO/CASCO work in this field is greatly helped by the discussions and studies that are taking place in such fora as the International Laboratory Accreditation Conference (ILAC) and the International Accreditation Forum (IAF), whose pre-standardisation work is pursued under ISO aegis each time a need for international consensus on a standard-type document is identified.

The usefulness of this work has been acknowledged in the successive GATT Agreements on Technical Barriers to Trade in which strong encouragement is given to all parties concerned to work directly at the international level whenever possible. A former Managing Director of the British Standards Institution used to repeat a phrase (called sometimes the "Feilden principle" by insiders): "Do it once, do it right, do it internationally!" This should remain everybody's objective, and I believe that the target is getting closer each year in many fields.

A typical example is that of the world-wide adoption of the ISO 9000 series of quality management standards, and the use that is made of these standards in establishing confidence in the competence of a producer of goods or services. We shall revert later to the international aspect of this matter, but I should like to echo the comment made yesterday by a Norwegian participant, and to stress with him that the assessment of a manufacturer's quality system is only a tool to provide a presumption of competence of that manufacturer to produce specific goods or services. It does not mean that the product itself has been assessed, and manufacturers are not allowed to publicise the ISO 9000 certification of their quality system in a way that could imply that their product has been certified (unless of course their product has actually been certified under a third-party product certification system, which is a different matter). Guidance in this respect is given in the ISO leaflet *Publicising your ISO 9000 registration.*

If one excepts phenomena such as the Woolmark, the only truly international programs in existence today are those operated by the IEC. These are: IECQ for the quality of electronic components, IECEE for the safety of household and similar appliances, and soon, IECE for equipment in explosive atmospheres. The second of these three IEC programs, the IECEE CB Scheme, has been quoted many times at this conference, notably in relation with the study on microwave ovens. According to information published by the IEC Secretariat and reported at the last meeting of ISO/CASCO, over 1000 manufacturers, located in 43 countries, are using the Scheme each year, and the yearly growth rate is between 30% and 40%. The number of test certificates issued under the scheme rose from some 3500 certificates in 1993 to nearly 5000 certificates in 1994.

A new development will be the planned extension of the IECEE CB Scheme, called the CB Full Certification Scheme (CB-FCS). This extension is an option to be exercised by participants in the CB

Scheme and by applicants under the same IECEE management structure. In addition to type testing, the CB-FCS will include assessment of the manufacturer's quality system, regular surveillance through inspection of the approved manufacturer's quality system and product quality plans, and audit testing of samples taken from the factory.

As implied in this description, ISO 9000 quality management standards should find a further application there, since the assessment of a manufacturer's quality system is not only an element of confidence in the manufacturer's self-declaration or in a second party decision to trust that manufacturer. It is also a building block in a full-fledged third-party product certification. This underlines the importance of the latest program launched by ISO in association with IEC under the name QSAR.

The ISO/IEC Quality System Assessment Recognition Program (QSAR) is based on peer evaluation among accreditation bodies. It is intended to achieve the following objective with respect to ISO 9000 series of quality management standards:

> *"When a supplier is certified by a participating certification body in the ISO/IEC QSAR Programme, the certificate issued should be recognised as being valid by his customers, regardless of the location of the certification body, the supplier or the customer."*

Such recognition by ISO/IEC is intended to be attained, in practice, as follows:

-- first, the supplier concerned will arrange to be assessed and have its quality system certified to ISO 9000 by a certification body which, itself, has been accredited by an accreditation body recognised, under the QSAR Program, as conforming to approved ISO/IEC criteria (normally developed within ISO/CASCO).

-- once certified, the supplier may, in compliance with ISO/IEC rules and guidelines for declaration of conformance to ISO 9000 standards, use the ISO/IEC QSAR logo in its representations to its world-wide base of customers, for example in reference to its certificate of compliance with one of the quality management standards of the ISO 9000 series, on letterheads, in general (not product specific) advertising, in contract negotiations, etc.

ISO/IEC Guides and the ISO leaflet *Publicising your ISO 9000 registration* offer guidance in this area.

Further information on QSAR can be found in a document, presented at the last ISO General Assembly in September 1995, bearing the reference ISO/IEC QSAR 41 (Rev.2), dated July 1995.

The success of QSAR will depend on the support and involvement of all parties concerned: accreditation bodies, certification bodies, manufactures and their clients. One most promising aspect is the important role that the International Accreditation Forum (IAF) is expected to play in conducting the peer evaluation process among participating accreditation bodies on behalf of the ISO/IEC QSAR Board. Other encouraging elements are the practical certification experience available at national, regional and international (IEC) levels, and the availability of internationally agreed criteria developed within ISO/CASCO and approved at national level as well as at regional level (the EN 45000 series of European standards).

Furthermore, the ISO/IEC QSAR Program, if successful, would certainly facilitate the achievement of some of the objectives pursued by the OECD Committee on Consumer Policy. In particular, it would have, indirectly, a positive influence on the objectives identified in the OECD study, even if we are still quite far from the ideal situation mentioned in the study, namely to have one day "to contend with one international safety standard, one international testing and certification procedure and one international safety mark."

Reference has been made in the discussions to recent developments in the fields of environmental management and sustained development, developments which, incidentally, are tangible signs that industry is taking its responsibilities very seriously and at the highest level. Mention has been made, in this connection, of the role of ISO and of the work in progress in ISO/TC 207, and of its relevance for consumers, notably with reference to eco-labelling (ISO/TC 207/SC 3). It is too early to predict if the ISO 14000 series of environmental management standards will generate a new, ISO 9000-like phenomenon, but it was interesting to hear that assessment of conformity to relevant international standards of the ISO 14000 are already introduced in national programs, and that steps are being taken to create, from the onset, favourable conditions for mutual recognition across borders.

Since confidence is to be the basis of the whole exercise, it is important to ensure transparency and proper information of consumers. On the positive side, I would mention that the ISO Information Network (ISONET) offers, through its national and regional ISONET centres (often associated with GATT Inquiry Points), information services now enhanced, at the ISO/IEC Information Centre in Geneva, by the *ISO On-line* service, accessible direct via Internet, on WWW server.

On a less positive side, I would point out that care should always be taken to avoid using words that might tend to deceive consumers. It is that spirit that ISO/IEC Guide 2 on general definitions (a document quoted in the OECD study) indicates that the old term "self-certification" should be abandoned and replaced by the term "supplier's declaration" (or manufacturer's declaration). It is a fact that the word certification has, in everybody's mind, a connotation of impartiality, which is out of place in the context. I know that it will take time before the old term disappears from all official documents in certain countries (maybe the somewhat redundant term *self-declaration* might help the transition in these countries), but I would hope that OECD could give the good example and clarify this point in the final version of their study – a study which we look forward to perusing again once finalised.

One welcomed statement, made by Mr. Ludolph and echoed later by Mr. Bhatia, was that it is necessary "to bring all interested parties around the table." This is precisely what the ISO/IEC system is constantly setting as a target. But the extent and the form in which this is achieved may vary from one sector to another and from one region to another – in particular with respect to the input of the experience available in insurance companies, to take the example given yesterday. It should be kept in mind that, however irreversible and prevailing the globalisation trend might be, we live in a world that is not yet ideal, as both Mr. Vaucelle and Mr. Repussard pointed out. This is why the efforts to take on board the views of all parties concerned will only have effective chances of success if they take place at all levels – and in the first place at national level.

To the question of the allocation of resources between harmonisation on the one hand, and mutual recognition agreement (MRA) negotiations on the other, I would be tempted to say: "why don't you join hands?!" Remembering however that the best MRA is the one you can do without (when the situation is so satisfactory that "it goes without saying"), the MRAs should, whenever possible, be based on internationally agreed criteria and be open to others. Observers from another (ideal) galaxy, if viewing our planet from afar, would certainly find it sometimes pathetic to see occasional traces of possible proliferation of MRAs, all painfully negotiated because they are based on the attitude "please wait until our documents are finalised, *i.e.* wait that our positions are well entrenched, then we will negotiate"!

To conclude, I believe we all agree that it is in the market place that the effective success of mutual recognition may be measured. We have seen that a lot has been done, but that a lot remains to be done. This OECD Conference is a most encouraging sign this effort will not be isolated, and that continued support and co-operation may be hoped for at all levels. The ISO and IEC Secretaries-General both asked me to convey to this conference their assurance that, for its part, the ISO/IEC international standardisation system, through its national members in some 115 countries, will continue to be ready to respond swiftly to the demands placed upon it.

John CLARKE

In 1994 the European Commission started negotiating mutual recognition agreements (MRAs) between the European Community and a number of third countries. I would like to explain what MRAs are, their objectives and potential benefits, and the elements necessary for mutual recognition to function successfully.

MRAs, in the sense I am using the term, are agreements on the mutual recognition of conformity assessment procedures for regulated products. Through an MRA, parties will have the right to test and certify their products to the requirements of the other party in their own territory and prior to export. Each party will recognise the tests, certificates, and marks of conformity delivered by recognised conformity assessment bodies in the other party. Products can then be placed on the market of the importing party without having to undergo further testing, certificates or approvals.

MRAs were originally conceived as a development from the Single European Market, and in particular in response to concerns over "Fortress Europe." Such concerns could be dispelled by allowing competent third country conformity assessment bodies to take part in EC conformity assessment activities. Beyond this however, MRAs are a way to facilitate trade and market access for regulated products. This is explicitly recognised in the World Trade Organisation Agreement on Technical Barriers to Trade, Article 6, which encourages the negotiation of MRAs between signatories of the Agreement.

MRAs apply to products regulated by the public authorities in the parties to the MRA, and not to what is popularly referred to as the "voluntary" sector. For this reason they must be negotiated and concluded between governments. The MRAs currently being negotiated by the European Community cover a range of regulated sectors, such as telecommunications equipment, electrical products, medical devices, pharmaceuticals, chemicals, and motor vehicles.

MRAs do not require prior harmonisation of the standards and technical regulations of the two parties to the MRA. Parties can test and certify to the other party's requirements whether they be different or the same: each party's individual "technical culture" is thus respected. Experience shows that harmonisation of product technical regulations takes longer to achieve. However, experience to date also indicates that mutual recognition agreements may be easier to achieve in sectors where regulations and standards have been harmonised or judged to be equivalent

The objectives and potential benefits of MRAs are as follows: First, MRAs benefit the consumer. An MRA can lead to a reduction of the costs and time taken to put a product on the market, to the benefit of economic operators and ultimately the consumer of the product. Figures are elusive, but one OECD survey of the telecommunications equipment sector estimated that at least 2 per cent of costs could be reduced by MRAs. Savings may be greater in more heavily regulated sectors. The savings gained through mutual recognition in the context of the European Single Market are well documented.

In terms of consumer protection, the consumer may also benefit through the more efficient allocation of resources by regulators; the possibility of more regular and systematic inspection and evaluation of products and processes by conformity assessment bodies located in the territory of production; and through the more systematic sharing of product information between government regulators who are implementing the agreements.

Second, MRAs can benefit the small- and medium-sized enterprise. SMEs may be more able to understand and access third country conformity assessment procedures though the medium of domestic conformity assessment bodies. At the moment larger companies, which are often established in the third countries, have a natural advantage when it comes to understanding or negotiating a way through that country's regulatory system. MRAs also help to reduce cost and time to have a product tested and approved for marketing in a third country. This is particularly important for products having a limited shelf life, where getting to the market quickly is a precondition for be able to successfully market the product. Reduction in cost and time obviously will lead to benefit for industry and exporters and ultimately to the consumers of the product

Third, MRAs can help regulatory agencies because they represent a form of "devolution" of regulatory activity which allows greater economic efficiency. Reliance on a partner's conformity assessment system enables limited domestic resources to be allocated to other regulatory objectives. In the EC's conception of mutual recognition, this is a strategic tool to stimulate deregulation because by definition, to achieve mutual recognition, each party has to devolve conformity assessment procedures to overseas testing and certification bodies.

If we take the classic situation in many countries, where the regulatory power is still in the hands of sole governmental agencies, mutual recognition constitutes an important deregulatory step. This might mean that the Ministry of Health, FDA, FCC, etc. would begin to relinquish its regulatory monopoly and begin to rely on the conformity assessment results performed by public or private bodies in third countries. Mutual recognition can also resolve some of the problems that potentially arise in situations where a certifying authority is, for reasons of industrial policy, acting in a manner which discriminates against foreign suppliers or where a certification body combines certification of imports with research on behalf of domestic industry, and where a conflict of interest, or concerns over technology transfer or abuse of intellectual property rights may arise.

Finally, MRAs can aid the process of harmonisation. Although, as noted above, mutual recognition need not depend on prior harmonisation of parties' standards and technical regulations, experience is beginning to show that MRA initiatives, along with other forms of regulatory co-operation, can create an important incentive for greater harmonisation.

Mutual recognition is no easy business, and we have experienced a number of major challenges in the European Community. The concept is often misunderstood to mean recognition of identical standards or equivalent regulations. But one does not have to have identical technical regulations to be able to negotiate mutual recognition. In any case, harmonisation of regulations, and mutual recognition of certification, are separate issues, each with their own merits. I can illustrate this by noting that even if two countries have harmonised their standards or technical requirements in a particular sector, this does not automatically mean that they will accept each others' certificates of conformity. That further step -- the necessary step to achieve market access of the product -- requires a mutual recognition agreement. It is also difficult to gain from industry detailed information on the certification systems, market access and technical barriers in third countries.

Another problem has been the difficulty in obtaining from industry a price on the cost of getting regulatory approvals in third countries. For this reason, I am grateful to what the OECD is doing in this area, which is an important step towards compiling quantitative data on the cost of getting products approved in third-country markets.

We have also encountered some difficulties in negotiating mutual recognition due to differences in the approach taken between the European Community and our negotiating partners. One problem has concerned the lack of transparency of some partner countries' standards and regulations, particularly where one is dealing with a sub-Federal system, where regulations may also be at the level of states, territories or municipalities. Clearly, if one wants to negotiate comprehensive agreements that improve market access and cover all certification procedures, it is very important to identify and negotiate access to regulatory rules at every level. Some third country partners have difficulties in persuading their regulatory agencies to delegate completely to the EC the authority to certify and approve products to their rules without any further intervention on the national regulator's part.

In conclusion, the following elements would seem to be necessary to ensure the successful operation of mutual recognition agreements:

-- mutual economic interest in respect to the products and sectors benefitting from mutual recognition, together with a shared perception of the trade, economic welfare and deregulatory benefits of mutual recognition over the long term;

-- the existence in each Party of standards and technical regulations which are both transparent and capable of correct interpretation and application by the other Party;

-- confidence in the competence of each Party's conformity assessment systems to operate to the other Party's requirements;

-- mechanisms for co-operation between the Parties to ensure that requirements continue to be applied uniformly, and appropriate safeguard measures in the event of failure to do so.

In Europe there are dozens of new ideas to improve conformity assessment procedures in various industries. The proliferation of these schemes creates difficulties for laboratories and certification bodies, who every day test many things with many different requirements. The bodies have the hard job of demonstrating that they are competent in these many areas. All this must be minimised and requires a horizontal approach, ideally with just have one assessment method.

The ultimate goal is a "world-wide one-stop testing and certification" for both the voluntary and the mandatory areas. To create a global marketplace for products, it is necessary to create a global marketplace for conformity assessment services. Harmonisation of legislation and an environment of confidence is required. According to the GATT/WTO Agreement accreditation is also an important tool for creation of confidence in certification and testing. How can this be done?

In the voluntary area, it is necessary to conclude bilateral and multilateral agreements between accreditation bodies. The European Community has now reached a multilateral agreement that covers eight countries, and laboratories have 12 members in multilateral agreements as well as bilateral agreements with Hong Kong, New Zealand, Australia, and South Africa, ensuring that test results from those countries will be accepted as well.

In the mandatory area, we must seek to harmonise legal requirements for competence and assessment methods, while at the same time ensuring harmony with requirements in the voluntary area. Ideally, this would incorporate national "voluntary" de facto marking and certification schemes, e.g. UL, GS, etc., into world-wide agreements. Globally, this requires agreement on a world-wide level concerning the methods, procedures and framework needed. This can be accomplished through bilateral mutual recognition agreements, multilateral agreements between "trading blocks," or multilateral agreements within the framework of GATT/WTO.

We must create the necessary infrastructure for mutual confidence (methods of assessment, requirements, etc.). This can be achieved through accreditation systems operated according to world-wide standards. We must also ensure that these systems are respected and enforced in an efficient and transparent manner.

To create a global marketplace, it is not enough to only harmonise standards. Legislation must also be harmonised or the commitment to use international standards must be made. To achieve the harmonisation of accreditation procedures and requirements a lot of work has to be done within the organisations for accreditation bodies. This work has the aim of establishing unified interpretation of standards and requirements in directives, legislation etc. The work has just started up in some sectors of the world, e.g. by EAC and EAL in Europe, but a lot remains to be done, especially on a world-wide basis.

This task is not an easy one. Different interests might create difficulties in the interpretation of the guiding documents. In order to achieve acceptance of the accreditation systems all interested parties have to be consulted, e.g. industry, consumers and governmental agencies.

One way of reaching these objectives is to create organisations of all interested parties for promotion of world-wide acceptance of certificates and test results. One example of such an organisation is ISO QSAR for acceptance of certification according to the ISO 9000 standards. Similar action is planned in the laboratory area.

Jacques REPUSSARD

Let us imagine an ideal world: In this world, applicable product and service specifications are well known by all economic participants active in that market, and all participants have equal access to the conformity assessment procedures that may exist in order to maintain a high level of protection in areas such as consumer protection, health and safety, and protection of the environment. Confidence of market operators in the quality of the work of the various conformity assessment organisations is largely based on the operation of the market itself and competition eliminates the less efficient operators. Accreditation systems are not seen as providing a licence to operate, but as a complementary objective tool to evaluate the reliability of assessment organisations such as laboratories and certification bodies. Mutual recognition does not need to be negotiated; mutual confidence in the reliability of market players of all kinds simply exists or it does not, and is determined by natural market mechanisms of selection and elimination.

The real world, however, is somewhat different. Not so much in the sense that it is not ideal -- an ideal world might be boring -- but because in the real world different "worlds" coexist whose relationships cannot for various reasons operate on the ideal model indicated above. The result is that those very mechanisms which were designed to ensure good functioning of the market in one part of the world sometimes became obstacles for market participants from other parts.

For fifty years, economic expansion has been nearly always based on a continuous development of international trade, hence policies aimed at further reducing what are commonly called technical barriers to trade. Such policies have been pursued both on regional levels (e.g. in Europe, in North America, or more recently in South America), and at the international level.

For Europe, it is interesting to note that from the outset, the objective was full harmonisation, leading to a single market operation. The consequence of this was that there was little use of the concept of mutual recognition. In fact, although mutual recognition was one of the alternatives foreseen in the "Acte Unique" which followed the Treaty of Rome to pave the way for the single market, this method was never used, and harmonisation was always seen as the preferable and most effective approach. The recent decision of CEN and CENELEC to launch a new European product certification mark also points in this way. EOTC's efforts to create a consensus among market participants in the area of conformity assessment will also eventually lead to a situation where market confidence will not need to be propped up by sometimes painfully negotiated recognition agreements.

It is important to remember that mutual recognition is a complex and time consuming process, and those who are involved with it are usually the same who could devote their resources to work on harmonisation objectives. This leads to the key question at the international level: what is the best course to develop necessary market fluidity?

At a recent conference in Seville, business leaders from Europe and the USA came to the conclusion that they would like to further reduce what they perceive to be technical barriers to trade.

Two possible courses lay ahead: one would clearly signal an ambition to harmonise, while the other would seek to establish mutual recognition mechanisms. The first course would lead to a reinforced commitment to develop international structures such as those of ISO/IEC, and to strengthen the use of international standards in domestic markets, as was done in Europe. The results may take some time, but once achieved they would achieve economic fluidity not just at a bilateral level, but on a global scale.

A decision to take the second course, and multiply bilateral negotiations aimed at mutual recognition, would, on the other hand, divert a notable share of available resources from the harmonisation objectives, without necessarily leading to satisfactory results. When two systems are quite different from one another, experience shows that mutual recognition of parts of these systems may simplify some operations in the short term, but does not radically change the long-term scenario. This explains the rather provocative title for this presentation: "Are mutual recognition policies a step towards harmonisation, or merely a diversion to delay it?"

Vivien LIU

Introduction

"Differing safety standards and costly conformity assessment requirements are major obstacles to trade in consumer products" as stated in the background document of this conference. The WTO Agreement on Technical Barriers to Trade was negotiated with the view to minimising these obstacles to trade.

After the Kennedy Round (1964-67) the Contracting Parties of the GATT started to address their concerns over non-tariff trade barriers, many of which related to differences in national standards and technical regulations. As a result, the Agreement on Technical Barriers to Trade was negotiated under the Tokyo Round and entered into force in January 1980. It laid emphasis on the use of harmonised, international product standards whenever possible, and set out new disciplines over the use of trade-related technical regulations not based on international standards.

The Uruguay Round negotiations expanded the TBT Agreement from a plurilateral agreement, with 47 Signatories from among the GATT Contracting Parties, into a multilateral agreement applicable to all WTO Members. The WTO TBT Agreement expanded its coverage to cover conformity assessment procedures, as defined in Annex 1 of the Agreement: "any procedure used, directly or indirectly, to determine that relevant requirements in technical regulations or standards are fulfilled," . . .including "inter alia, procedures for sampling, testing and inspection, evaluation, verification and assurance of conformity; registration, accreditation and approval as well as their combinations." Existing disciplines on the preparation, adoption and application of technical regulations, standards and procedures for assessment of conformity to avoid the creation of unnecessary obstacles to trade were improved and expanded. Additional disciplines were provided for local government regulatory activities. The Code of Good Practice for the Preparation, Adoption and Application of Standards contained in Annex 3 of the Agreement extends many of the disciplines of the Agreement to voluntary standards set by central governments, local governments, non-governmental and regional standardising bodies.

Main Disciplines of the WTO Agreement on Technical Barriers to Trade

1. Non-discrimination

Article 2.1, Article 5.1 and paragraph D of the Code of Good Practice contain disciplines of national treatment and MFN treatment. Technical regulations, standards and procedures for conformity assessment shall be applied to products imported from other WTO Members in a manner no less favourable than that accorded to like products of national origin and to like products originating in any other country.

2. Avoidance of unnecessary obstacles to trade

While recognising in its Preambular language that no country should be prevented from taking measures necessary to achieve a number of public policy objectives, including the protection of consumers, animal or plant life or health or the environment, at the levels it considers appropriate, the TBT Agreement obliges Members to ensure that their technical regulations, standards and procedures for conformity assessment are not prepared, adopted or applied with a view to, or with the effect of, creating unnecessary obstacles to trade.

Article 2.2 elaborates this discipline for technical regulations, which shall not be more trade-restrictive than necessary to fulfil a legitimate objective, taking into account the risks non-fulfilment would create. In addition, technical regulations shall not be maintained if the circumstances or objectives giving rise to their adoption no longer exist or if the changed circumstances or objectives can be addressed in a less trade-restrictive manner.

Similar clarification for conformity assessment procedures is provided in Article 5. They shall not be more strict or be applied more strictly than is necessary to give the importing Member adequate confidence that products conform with technical regulations or standards. Members shall ensure that conformity assessment procedures are undertaken and completed as expeditiously as possible, that information requirements are limited to what is necessary to assess conformity, and that the siting of facilities used to assess conformity are not such as to cause unnecessary inconvenience to applicants. Article 8 of the Agreement obliges Members to take such reasonable measures as may be available to them to ensure that non-governmental bodies within their territories which operate conformity assessment procedures observe these disciplines.

3. Encouraging harmonisation

In order to minimise obstacles to trade that could be created by national differences in technical regulations, standards and procedures for conformity assessment, the TBT Agreement strongly encourages harmonisation through the use of international standards and guides unless this would be ineffective or inappropriate to national needs, the acceptance of the technical regulations of other Members as equivalent, and mutual recognition of conformity assessment procedures by central government bodies.

(i)   Harmonisation through international standards

With a view to reducing unnecessary obstacles to trade and improving economic efficiency, Members are encouraged to use relevant international standards or guides as a basis for harmonising their technical regulations, standards and conformity assessment procedures on as wide a basis as possible, and to participate in the work of international standardising bodies. A technical regulation which is prepared in accordance with relevant international standards is rebuttably presumed not to create an unnecessary obstacle to international trade. The Code of Good Practice also encourages standardising bodies to avoid duplication in their work at the national, regional and international levels.

(ii)   The principle of equivalence

Article 2.7 of the TBT Agreement encourages Members to give positive consideration to accepting other Members' technical regulations as equivalent, provided they are satisfied that these regulations adequately fulfil the policy objectives of their own regulations.

(iii)   Mutual recognition of conformity assessment procedures

Multiple testing, inspection and certification of products exported to different countries increases business costs and uncertainties and can create unnecessary barriers to trade. Ideally, testing of a product should take place only once in the country of origin and the test results should be accepted in all export markets.

Article 6 of the TBT Agreement encourages Members to enter into negotiations for mutual recognition agreements on conformity assessment and to accept the results of conformity assessment procedures in other Members whenever possible, provided they are satisfied with those procedures and that they offer an assurance of conformity equivalent to their own procedures. The Agreement recognises that prior consultations may be necessary in order to arrive at a mutually satisfactory understanding regarding the competence of the relevant conformity assessment bodies. In that connection, relevant guides or recommendations issued by international standardising bodies are to be taken into account as an indication of adequate technical competence.

4.   Transparency Provisions

Transparency is viewed as an important means to build confidence in and provide security and stability to the multilateral trading system, to help minimise the risk of trade restriction and distortion from arising, to assist the private sector to adjust to changing trade policies, and to prevent misunderstandings and ultimately trade disputes from occurring. Considerable importance is therefore attached by the TBT Agreement to ensuring that advance knowledge of technical regulations, standards and conformity assessment procedures is available to all WTO Members. The

Agreement creates two transparency obligations: a passive approach of setting up enquiry points, and an active approach of submitting notifications.

(i) Enquiry points

Each Member is required to ensure that a national enquiry point exists which is able to answer all reasonable enquiries from other Members regarding its technical regulations, standards and conformity assessment procedures and also to provide relevant documentation.

(ii) Notifications

If the technical regulations or procedures for conformity assessment prepared by Members are not the same as or are not based substantially on international standards, and if they may have a significant effect on the trade of other Members, they must be notified to other Members through the WTO Secretariat at a sufficiently early stage in their drafting (generally at least 60 days prior to their formal adoption) so as to allow reasonable time for other Members to make comments. Members are required to take the comments into account before adopting the regulations or conformity assessment procedures and publishing them.

In the case of standards, standardising bodies which accept the Code of Good Practice for the Preparation, Adoption and Application of Standards are required to notify their work programmes through the ISO/IEC Information Centre so that interested parties can be informed of the standards they are preparing. They are also required to take into account comments received when further processing the standards.

Conclusion

Technical regulations, standards and conformity assessment procedures remain an important source of non-tariff trade barriers. The disciplines of the WTO TBT Agreement seek to ensure that these trade barriers can be minimised. Full implementation of the TBT Agreement by WTO Members will provide some answers to concerns of producers and consumers that "differing safety standards and costly conformity assessment requirements are major obstacles to trade in consumer products." WTO Members are obliged to provide non-discrimination treatments and avoid unnecessary obstacles to trade when preparing, adopting and applying technical regulations, standards and conformity assessment procedures. Moreover, international standards and guides should be adopted by Members as much as possible and governments should follow the principle of accepting as "equivalent" different national regulations. Members should reach mutual recognition agreements (MRAs) on conformity assessment procedures with other Members to avoid problems of costly re-testing and certification requirements.

In connection with that, Article 10.7 of the Agreement requires Members to notify other Members on agreements they reach with any other country relating to standards or conformity assessment procedures. Members concerned are encouraged to enter, upon request, into consultations with other Members for the purposes of concluding similar agreements or of arranging for their participation in such agreements. This provision could be used as a base to broaden the reach and extend the benefits of bilateral or plurilateral mutual recognition agreements in the multilateral trading system. The TBT Agreement encourages the development of international conformity assessment systems and Article 9 of the Agreement encourages Members to formulate and adopt international systems for conformity assessment and become members thereof or participate therein where a positive assurance of conformity with a technical regulation or standard is required. In this respect international conformity assessment systems can be regarded as a long term contribution to improving the efficiency and facilitating the conduct of international trade.

After fully implementing the new obligations undertaken through the Uruguay Round, WTO Members may start thinking of further improving the disciplines of the TBT Agreement. One of the issues which might warrant attention is that the TBT provisions regarding harmonisation (e.g. harmonisation through international standards, accepting other Members' technical regulations as equivalent, mutual recognition of conformity assessment procedures, expanding MRAs with other Members and formulating international systems for conformity assessment) provide only weak "encouragement" obligations. WTO Members might consider whether there is a need to strengthen those provisions in order to further facilitate international trade.

The WTO TBT Agreement imposes obligations on governments. However, it provides benefits for producers, exporters and consumers. Members should take care that producers and other interested parties within their territories make full use of the transparency provisions of the Agreement. It is the interest of consumers if producers can benefit from the TBT Agreement so that the negative trade effects of the proliferation of different national standards and requirements of re-testing and re-certifying of products can be minimised. The ultimate aim of the trading system is to provide consumers with a wide choice of high quality products at competitive prices.

Annex 1

THE OECD SURVEY

Table 1				Table 2		

Manufacturer responses by country and region   Trade association responses by country and region

	# of responses	% of total responses		# of responses	% of total responses
Denmark	3	3%	France	2	15%
Finland	3	3%	Sweden	1	8%
France	3	3%	United Kingdom	2	15%
Germany	17	18%	**Europe**	**5**	**38%**
Greece	2	2%			
Italy	4	4%	Mexico	1	8%
Netherlands	2	2%	United States	4	31%
Portugal	2	2%	**North America**	**5**	**38%**
Sweden	4	4%			
United Kingdom	24	25%	Japan	3	23%
Europe	**64**	**67%**	**Asia-Pacific**	**3**	**23%**
Mexico	3	3%	**TOTAL**	**13**	**100%**
United States	14	15%			
North America	**17**	**18%**			
Australia	1	1%			
Japan	15	14%			
Asia-Pacific	**14**	**15%**			
TOTAL	**95**	**100%**			

Table 3

Table 4

Manufacturer responses by product category			Trade association responses by product category		
	# of responses	*% of total responses*		*# of responses*	*% of total responses*
Toys	58	61%	Toys	5	38%
Microwave Ovens	8	8%	Microwave Ovens	3	23%
Lawn Mowers	22	23%	Lawn Mowers	4	31%
Bicycle Helmets	7	7%	Bicycle Helmets	1	8%
TOTAL	**95**	**100%**	**TOTAL**	**13**	**100%**

| | Table 5 | | Table 6 | | |

Responses from toy manufacturers by country and region

Responses from microwave oven manufacturers by country and region

	# of responses	% of total responses		# of responses	% of total responses
Denmark	1	2%	Germany	1	14%
Finland	3	5%	Japan	4	57%
France	1	2%	United States	3	29%
Germany	6	10%			
Greece	2	3%	**TOTAL**	**8**	**100%**
Italy	4	7%			
Netherlands	2	3%			
Portugal	2	3%			
Sweden	1	2%			
United Kingdom	22	38%			
Europe	**44**	**76%**			
Mexico	1	2%			
United States	8	14%			
North America	**9**	**16%**			
Australia	1	2%			
Japan	4	7%			
Asia-Pacific	**5**	**9%**			
TOTAL	**58**	**100%**			

Table 7   **Table 8**

Responses from lawn mower manufacturers by country and region

	# of responses	% of total responses
Denmark	2	9%
France	1	5%
Germany	7	32%
Sweden	2	9%
United Kingdom	2	9%
Europe	**14**	**64%**
Mexico	1	5%
United States	2	9%
North America	**3**	**14%**
Japan	5	23%
Asia-Pacific	**5**	**23%**
TOTAL	**22**	**100%**

Responses from bicycle helmet manufacturers by country and region

	# of responses	% of total responses
France	1	14%
Germany	3	43%
Sweden	1	14%
Europe	**5**	**71%**
Mexico	1	14%
United States	1	14%
North America	**2**	**29%**
TOTAL	**7**	**100%**

Table 9

Size of respondent manufacturers based on total annual sales for all products manufactured by respondents

Size	# of responses	% of total responses
Small (US$ 0 - 10 million)	36	46%
Medium (US$ 10 - 100 million)	22	28%
Large (US$ 100 million +)	21	27%
TOTAL	**79**	**100%**

Table 10

Size of respondent manufacturers by region

Region	Small	Medium	Large
Europe	27	18	7
North America	5	3	8
Asia-Pacific	4	1	6
TOTAL	**36**	**22**	**21**

Table 11

Number of respondent trade association members that manufacture products surveyed

Country	Total	Small- and medium-sized	Large
Japan	511	498	13
Mexico	120	120	
Sweden	3	2	1
United Kingdom	220	210	10
United States	235	225	10
TOTAL	**1089**	**1055**	**34**

Note: Some respondents did not provide details about members.

Table 12

Table 13

Countries where respondent manufacturers manufacture their products	# of responses	% of total responses
European Union	9	9%
Austria	2	2%
Belgium	1	1%
Denmark	5	5%
Finland	3	3%
France	7	7%
Germany	17	18%
Greece	2	2%
Ireland		
Italy	9	9%
Netherlands	1	1%
Norway	1	1%
Portugal	3	3%
Spain	4	4%
Sweden	5	5%
Switzerland	3	3%
United Kingdom	24	25%
Canada	1	1%
Mexico	12	13%
United States	22	23%
Australia	2	2%
Japan	12	13%
Brazil	7	7%
China	25	26%
India	1	1%

Countries where respondent trade association members manufacture their products	# of responses	% of total responses
European Union	6	46%
Austria		
Belgium	2	15%
Denmark	1	8%
Finland	1	8%
France	5	38%
Germany	4	31%
Greece	1	8%
Ireland	2	15%
Italy	2	15%
Netherlands	1	8%
Norway		
Portugal		
Spain	1	8%
Sweden	3	23%
Switzerland	1	8%
United Kingdom	3	23%
Canada	4	31%
Mexico	5	38%
United States	7	54%
Australia	2	15%
Japan	8	62%
Brazil	4	31%
China	5	38%
India	1	8%

99

Table 14			Table 15		
Countries where respondent manufacturers sell their products			**Countries where respondent trade association members sell their products**		
	# of responses	*% of total responses*		*# of responses*	*% of total responses*
European Union	61	64%	European Union	12	92%
Austria	58	61%	Austria	9	69%
Belgium	67	71%	Belgium	9	69%
Denmark	62	65%	Denmark	9	69%
Finland	52	55%	Finland	7	54%
France	71	75%	France	9	69%
Germany	72	76%	Germany	9	69%
Greece	47	49%	Greece	7	54%
Iceland	41	43%	Iceland	8	62%
Ireland	57	60%	Ireland	8	62%
Italy	56	59%	Italy	9	69%
Luxembourg	45	47%	Luxembourg	8	62%
Netherlands	64	67%	Netherlands	9	69%
Norway	61	64%	Norway	11	85%
Portugal	51	54%	Portugal	8	62%
Spain	55	58%	Spain	8	62%
Sweden	62	65%	Sweden	9	69%
Switzerland	61	64%	Switzerland	10	77%
Turkey	26	27%	Turkey	8	62%
United Kingdom	71	75%	United Kingdom	9	69%
Canada	50	53%	Canada	10	77%
Mexico	35	37%	Mexico	8	62%
United States	57	60%	United States	12	92%
Australia	53	56%	Australia	9	69%
Japan	46	48%	Japan	9	69%
New Zealand	45	47%	New Zealand	9	69%
Brazil	28	29%	Brazil	7	54%
China	19	20%	China	6	46%
India	13	14%	India	4	31%
Russia	27	28%	Russia	5	38%

Table 16

Safety standards applicable in most important markets where respondent manufacturers sell their products

5 most frequently cited markets	# of responses	5 most frequently cited standards	# of responses	The standard is mandatory	The standard is voluntary	The standard is both voluntary and mandatory
European Union	31	ASTM	10	3	5	3
Germany	13	CE	11	9	5	2
Japan	5	EN 71	45	34	4	8
United Kingdom	23	EN 836	8	2	6	
United States	20	HD 271	11	9	1	2

Table 17

Safety standards applicable to products in most important markets where respondent trade association members sell their products

4 most frequently cited markets	# of responses	4 most frequently cited standards	# of responses	The standard is mandatory	The standard is voluntary	The standard is both voluntary and mandatory
European Union	8	ASTM F963	3		1	
Japan	1	CPSC	2		1	1
United Kingdom	1	EN 71	4	2		2
United States	7	IEC 335-2-25	2	2		

Table 18

Reasons why respondent manufacturers' products conform to voluntary safety standards

	strongly agree	agree somewhat	neither agree nor disagree	disagree somewhat	strongly disagree
Products conform to voluntary safety standards because end consumers demand it.	17	26	12	6	1
Products conform to voluntary safety standards because distributors/importers demand it.	29	21	5	6	
Conformance to voluntary safety standards improves the quality of these products.	27	21	7	4	3
Conformance to voluntary safety standards reduces safety risks for consumers.	33	19	8	2	
Conformance to voluntary safety standards reduces official barriers to sell these products.	30	21	4	3	4
Conformance to voluntary safety standards reduces the risk of legal liability.	33	13	9	2	3
Conformance to voluntary safety standards helps to protect the respondent's reputation.	38	18	2	4	

Table 19

Reasons why respondent trade association's products conform to voluntary safety standards

	strongly agree	agree somewhat	neither agree nor disagree	disagree somewhat	strongly disagree
Products conform to voluntary safety standards because end consumers demand it.	4	2	3		1
Products conform to voluntary safety standards because distributors/importers demand it.	5	3	2		
Conformance to voluntary safety standards improves the quality of these products.	3	2	3	1	
Conformance to voluntary safety standards reduces safety risks for consumers.	7	2		1	
Conformance to voluntary safety standards reduces official barriers to sell these products.	7	2		1	
Conformance to voluntary safety standards reduces the risk of legal liability.	6	3		1	
Conformance to voluntary safety standards helps to protect the respondent's reputation.	7	3			

Table 20

In markets where respondent manufacturers already sell, manufacturing to the relevant standard significantly increases costs

	strongly agree	agree somewhat	neither agree nor disagree	disagree somewhat	strongly disagree
European Union	17	36	7	4	3
Austria	7	22	12	5	1
Belgium	9	27	11	6	2
Denmark	12	22	11	5	
Finland	8	18	8	3	1
France	12	27	9	5	2
Germany	13	26	10	9	1
Greece	8	18	9	3	1
Iceland	7	11	10	4	1
Ireland	10	19	10	4	1
Italy	9	22	10	4	2
Luxembourg	8	17	9	3	1
Netherlands	10	23	11	6	1
Norway	9	22	12	4	2
Portugal	9	18	9	5	1
Spain	8	22	11	5	1
Sweden	11	22	9	6	
Switzerland	13	20	12	3	2
Turkey	6	9	8	2	
United Kingdom	17	24	7	6	2
Europe	**186**	**389**	**188**	**88**	**22**
Canada	12	16	6	5	3
Mexico	8	7	6	1	4
United States	10	23	10	6	3
North America	**30**	**46**	**22**	**12**	**10**
Australia	8	25	6	4	3
Japan	6	16	7	6	3
New Zealand	6	20	6	3	2
Asia-Pacific	**20**	**61**	**19**	**13**	**8**
Brazil	3	8	5	3	2
China	3	3	5	4	1
India	2	1	4	1	1
Russia	4	5	7	3	4
TOTAL	**265**	**549**	**257**	**128**	**51**

Table 21

In markets where respondent trade association members already sell, manufacturing to the relevant standard significantly increases costs

	strongly agree	agree somewhat	neither agree nor disagree	disagree somewhat	strongly disagree
European Union	2	7			
Austria	2	2	1		
Belgium	2	2	1		
Denmark	2	2	1		
Finland	2	2	1		
France	2	2	1		
Germany	2	2	1		
Greece	2	2	1		
Iceland	2	2	1		
Ireland	2	2	1		
Italy	2	2	1		
Luxembourg	2	2	1		
Netherlands	2	2	1		
Norway	2	3	1		
Portugal	2	2	1		
Spain	2	2	1		
Sweden	2	2	1		
Switzerland	2	3	1		
Turkey	2	3	1		
United Kingdom	2	2	1		
Europe	**38**	**41**	**19**		
Canada		3	3		
Mexico	1	2	3		
United States		2	3		
North America	**1**	**7**	**9**		
Australia	1	5	1		
Japan	1	3	1		
New Zealand	1	4	2		
Asia-Pacific	**3**	**12**	**4**		
Brazil		3	2		
China		3	1		
India		1	2		
Russia		4	1		
TOTAL	**44**	**78**	**38**	**0**	**0**

Table 22

In markets where respondent manufacturers already sell, manufacturing to the relevant standard significantly reduces ability to get new products to market quickly					
	strongly agree	*agree somewhat*	*neither agree nor disagree*	*disagree somewhat*	*strongly disagree*
European Union	9	17	13	9	11
Austria	4	9	15	7	6
Belgium	6	11	15	8	7
Denmark	8	11	15	7	4
Finland	6	11	9	5	2
France	7	13	13	7	11
Germany	15	15	9	11	8
Greece	4	8	13	5	6
Iceland	4	7	9	7	3
Ireland	4	9	14	7	7
Italy	5	10	13	6	7
Luxembourg	4	7	14	4	6
Netherlands	6	9	15	9	6
Norway	7	10	14	7	6
Portugal	5	9	13	7	7
Spain	4	9	13	8	7
Sweden	7	11	14	6	5
Switzerland	8	13	10	8	8
Turkey	3	5	6	5	3
United Kingdom	8	13	10	10	8
Europe	**115**	**190**	**234**	**134**	**117**
Canada	4	10	12	7	5
Mexico	4	4	8	3	3
United States	6	17	12	9	5
North America	**14**	**31**	**32**	**19**	**13**
Australia	4	11	11	10	6
Japan	2	10	6	11	5
New Zealand	3	8	10	9	3
Asia-Pacific	**9**	**29**	**27**	**30**	**14**
Brazil	1	5	6	3	4
China	1	3	3	4	4
India	1	2	2	2	3
Russia	1	6	5	5	4
TOTAL	**151**	**283**	**322**	**206**	**170**

Table 23

In markets where respondent trade association members already sell, manufacturing to the relevant standard significantly reduces ability to get new products to market quickly

	strongly agree	agree somewhat	neither agree nor disagree	disagree somewhat	strongly disagree
European Union	1	4	1	1	
Austria	1	1	1		
Belgium	1	1	1		
Denmark	1	1	1		
Finland	1	1	1		
France	1	1	1		
Germany	1	1	1		
Greece	1	1	1		
Iceland	1	1	1		
Ireland	1	1	1		
Italy	1	1	1		
Luxembourg	1	1	1		
Netherlands	1	1	1		
Norway	1	1	1	1	
Portugal	1	1	1		
Spain	1	1	1		
Sweden	1	1	1		
Switzerland	1	1	1	1	
Turkey	1	1	1	1	
United Kingdom	1	1	1		
Europe	**19**	**19**	**19**	**3**	
Canada		1	2	1	
Mexico		1	2	1	
United States		1	2	1	
North America		**3**	**6**	**3**	
Australia		1	2	2	
Japan		1	1	1	
New Zealand		1	2	2	
Asia-Pacific		**3**	**5**	**5**	
Brazil		1	2		
China		1	2		
India		1	2		
Russia		1	3		
TOTAL	**20**	**33**	**40**	**12**	**0**

Table 24

In markets where respondent manufacturers would like to sell, manufacturing to the relevant standard significantly would increase costs

	strongly agree	agree somewhat	neither agree nor disagree	disagree somewhat	strongly disagree
European Union	4	3	2	1	3
Austria		3	3	2	
Belgium		4	2	1	
Denmark		5	2	2	2
Finland		6	3	2	1
France	1	3	3	1	
Germany	2	3	2	1	
Greece		3	4	2	1
Iceland		4	8	2	
Ireland		3	3	1	
Italy		3	3	3	
Luxembourg		2	4	1	
Netherlands		4	3	1	
Norway		2	5	2	
Portugal		3	3	1	
Spain		2	3	1	1
Sweden		5	2	2	
Switzerland		4	3	1	
Turkey		3	7	3	1
United Kingdom		4	3	1	
Europe	**3**	**66**	**66**	**30**	**6**
Canada	4	8	5		
Mexico	2	4	2	1	1
United States	6	5	3		2
North America	**12**	**17**	**10**	**1**	**3**
Australia		3	4		
Japan		6	5		
New Zealand		3	4		1
Asia-Pacific		**12**	**13**		**1**
Brazil	2	2	6		1
China		4	6	2	2
India		6	7	1	1
Russia	3	4	6	1	
TOTAL	**24**	**114**	**116**	**36**	**17**

Table 25

In markets where respondent trade association members would like to sell, manufacturing to the relevant standard significantly would increase costs

	strongly agree	agree somewhat	neither agree nor disagree	disagree somewhat	strongly disagree
European Union		1			
Austria		1			
Belgium		1			
Denmark		1			
Finland		1			
France		1			
Germany		1			
Greece		1			
Iceland		1			
Ireland		1			
Italy		1			
Luxembourg		1			
Netherlands		1			
Norway		1			
Portugal		1			
Spain		1			
Sweden		1			
Switzerland		1			
Turkey		1			
United Kingdom		1			
Europe		**19**			
Canada	1	1	1		
Mexico		1			
United States	1	1			
North America	**2**	**3**	**1**		
Australia			1		
Japan					
New Zealand			1		
Asia-Pacific			**2**		
TOTAL	**2**	**23**	**3**	**0**	**0**

109

Table 26

In markets where respondent manufacturers would like to sell, manufacturing to the relevant standard significantly would reduce ability to get new products to market quickly

	strongly agree	agree somewhat	neither agree nor disagree	disagree somewhat	strongly disagree
European Union	2	3	4	2	2
Austria		4	3	1	
Belgium		4	2	1	
Denmark		4	2	1	3
Finland		3	4	1	4
France		3	2	3	
Germany	1	4	2	1	
Greece		3	3	2	2
Iceland		3	7	1	3
Ireland		3	2	1	1
Italy		2	3	4	
Luxembourg		3	2	2	
Netherlands		4	2	2	
Norway		3	4	1	1
Portugal		2	3	2	
Spain		2	2	2	1
Sweden		3	3	1	1
Switzerland		4	2	2	
Turkey		4	5	4	2
United Kingdom		2	2	2	1
Europe	**1**	**60**	**55**	**34**	**19**
Canada		5	3	4	2
Mexico		2	3	2	3
United States	2	3	3	2	3
North America	**2**	**10**	**9**	**8**	**8**
Australia		2	2	1	2
Japan	1	3	3	2	2
New Zealand		1	3	1	3
Asia-Pacific	**1**	**6**	**8**	**4**	**7**
Brazil	2	1	4	1	3
China		6	4	1	4
India		6	5	2	2
Russia	2	3	4	2	3
TOTAL	**10**	**95**	**93**	**54**	**48**

Table 27

In markets where respondent trade association members would like to sell, manufacturing to the relevant standard significantly would reduce ability to get new products to market quickly

	strongly agree	agree somewhat	neither agree nor disagree	disagree somewhat	strongly disagree
European Union			1		
Austria			1		
Belgium			1		
Denmark			1		
Finland			1		
France			1		
Germany			1		
Greece			1		
Iceland			1		
Ireland			1		
Italy			1		
Luxembourg			1		
Netherlands			1		
Norway			1		
Portugal			1		
Spain			1		
Sweden			1		
Switzerland			1		
Turkey			1		
United Kingdom			1		
Europe			**19**		
Canada		1	1		
Mexico			1		
United States			1		
North America		**1**	**3**		
Australia			1		
Japan					
New Zealand			1		
Asia-Pacific			**2**		
Brazil		1			
China		1			
India		1			
Russia		1			
TOTAL	**0**	**5**	**25**	**0**	**0**

111

Table 28

Reasons why respondent manufacturers decided to participate in the development of particular safety standards

	strongly agree	agree somewhat	neither agree nor disagree	disagree somewhat	strongly disagree
Participating in the development of this standard was a priority for the respondent.	29	18	6	2	1
The respondent believed that participation in the development of the standard would have a positive effect on the resulting standard.	30	21	5	1	
The costs of participation were reasonable for a company of the respondent's size.	19	15	14	6	1
If the respondent did not participate, its views might not have been heard.	30	13	8	2	
The respondent believed that the procedures of the standards development institution were basically fair.	13	24	9	9	1
The respondent was able to follow the procedural steps of the process without much difficulty.	15	26	4	6	3

Table 29

Reasons why respondent manufacturers decided to participate in the development of particular safety standards

	strongly agree	agree somewhat	neither agree nor disagree	disagree somewhat	strongly disagree
Participating in the development of this standard was a priority for the respondent's trade association.	8	3	1		
The respondent's trade association believed that participation in the development of the standard would have a positive effect on the resulting standard.	9	3			
The costs of participation were reasonable for an association of the respondent's size.	6	3	3		
If the respondent's trade association did not participate, its views might not have been heard.	6	3	3		
The respondent's trade association believed that the procedures of the standards development institution were basically fair.	5	5	2		
The respondent's trade association was able to follow the procedural steps of the process without much difficulty.	5	5	2		

Table 30

Reasons why respondent manufacturers decided not to participate in the development of standards

	strongly agree	agree somewhat	neither agree nor disagree	disagree somewhat	strongly disagree
Participating in the development of this standard was not a priority for the respondent.	7	10	16	3	19
The respondent believed that it could live with the standard that was likely to result even without its participation.	8	16	12	7	11
The costs of participation were too high for a company of the respondent's size.	9	7	18	10	11
The costs of participation were too high in light of the company's sales.	10	6	18	9	12
The respondent was not permitted to participate in the process.	15	7	16	5	12
The respondent believed that it was inappropriate to try to influence the development of this standard.	3	7	16	8	20
The respondent believed that the procedures of the standards development institution were unfair.	5	5	17	7	19
The respondent's views were already well enough represented.	3	7	16	11	18
The respondent was unaware that the standard was being developed.	13	7	7	10	21
The respondent did not believe that its input would have much of an effect on the final standard.	13	14	11	5	11

Table 31

Reasons why respondent trade associations decided not to participate in the development of standards

	strongly agree	agree somewhat	neither agree nor disagree	disagree somewhat	strongly disagree
Participating in the development of this standard was not a priority for the respondent.			1	1	1
The respondent believed that it could live with the standard that was likely to result even without its participation.		2			1
The costs of participation were too high for a company of the respondent's size.		1	1		1
The costs of participation were too high in light of the company's sales.	1			1	1
The respondent was not permitted to participate in the process.	1		1		1
The respondent believed that it was inappropriate to try to influence the development of this standard.			1	1	1
The respondent believed that the procedures of the standards development institution were unfair.			1	1	1
The respondent's views were already well enough represented.			1	1	1
The respondent was unaware that the standard was being developed.		1		1	1
The respondent did not believe that its input would have much of an effect on the final standard.			2		1

Table 32

**Most important markets where respondent manufacturers are already selling
and type of conformity assessment process required for that market**

---

5 most frequently cited countries	# of responses	Manufacturer self-declaration of conformance	Testing and certification by a government agency	Testing and certification by a government designated body	Testing and certification by non-government bodies
France	6	3	2	3	1
European Union	22	13	1	16	9
Germany	11	4		8	1
United Kingdom	19	7	1	5	12
United States	21	12	2	1	13

Table 33

**Most important markets where respondent trade associations are already selling
and type of conformity assessment process required for that market**

---

3 most frequently cited countries	# of responses	Manufacturer self-declaration of conformance	Testing and certification by a government agency	Testing and certification by a government designated body	Testing and certification by non-government bodies
European Union	3	2		1	
United Kingdom	2	1		1	
United States	3	1			3

Table 34

Reasons why respondent manufacturers voluntarily chose particular testing and certification procedures

	strongly agree	agree somewhat	neither agree nor disagree	disagree somewhat	strongly disagree
These procedures were used because end consumers demand them.	12	16	12	6	3
These procedures were used because distributors and/or importers demand them.	27	16	5	1	
Use of these procedures ensures the quality of the product.	21	23	5	2	1
Use of these procedures reduces safety risks to consumers.	26	19	5	2	
Use of these procedures reduces official barriers to sell the product in this market.	31	10	6	2	3
Use of these procedures reduces the risk of legal liability for a company.	23	18	6	2	
Use of these procedures helps to protect a company's reputation.	27	18	3	3	

Table 35

Reasons why respondent trade associations voluntarily chose particular testing and certification procedures

	strongly agree	agree somewhat	neither agree nor disagree	disagree somewhat	strongly disagree
These procedures were used because end consumers demand them.	1	2	1	3	2
These procedures were used because distributors and/or importers demand them.	3	2	3	1	
Use of these procedures ensures the quality of the product.	2	3	1	2	
Use of these procedures reduces safety risks to consumers.	5	3		1	
Use of these procedures reduces official barriers to sell the product in this market.	6	1	1	1	1
Use of these procedures reduces the risk of legal liability for a company.	4	3			2
Use of these procedures helps to protect a company's reputation.	4	2	2	1	

Table 36

What respondent manufacturers believe that a particular certification mark means to consumers

5 most frequently cited certification marks	# of responses	The product conforms to all government safety standards	The product meets high quality standards	The product is permitted to be sold on certain markets	The product is safe	The product meets the standards of a respected standards body	Consumers generally do not have any idea what the mark signifies
CE Mark	53	31	25	15	31	19	17
EN 71	8	5	4	2	8	4	3
GS standard	5	3	5		3	1	
TÜV	4	4	3	1	2	2	1
VDE	4	2	2	2	4	2	
UL	1	1	1	1	1	1	

Table 37

What respondent trade associations believe that a particular certification mark means to consumers

5 most frequently cited certification marks	# of responses	The product conforms to all government safety standards	The product meets high quality standards	The product is permitted to be sold on certain markets	The product is safe	The product meets the standards of a respected standards body	Consumers generally do not have any idea what the mark signifies
CE Mark	3	1			1		3
BS Kitemark	1		1		1	1	
ST (Toy Safety)	1	1	1		1	1	

Table 38	Table 39

Countries that respondent manufacturers believe require ISO 9000 (or a similar series of standards) registration of manufacturer facilities		**Countries that respondent trade associations believe require ISO 9000 (or a similar series of standards) registration of manufacturer facilities**	
	# of responses		*# of responses*
European Union	11	European Union	
Austria	3	Austria	
Belgium	2	Belgium	
Denmark	2	Denmark	
Finland	1	Finland	
France	2	France	
Germany	4	Germany	1
Greece	1	Greece	
Iceland	2	Iceland	
Ireland	2	Ireland	
Italy	2	Italy	
Luxembourg	2	Luxembourg	
Netherlands	2	Netherlands	
Norway	4	Norway	
Portugal	2	Portugal	
Spain	2	Spain	1
Sweden	2	Sweden	
Switzerland	3	Switzerland	
Turkey		Turkey	
United Kingdom	8	United Kingdom	
Canada	5	Canada	1
Mexico	1	Mexico	
United States	7	United States	1
Australia	2	Australia	
Japan	3	Japan	
Brazil		Brazil	1
China	1	China	1

Table 40

In countries where respondent manufacturers already sell, testing and certification to satisfy conformity assessment requirements significantly increase costs				
	strongly agree	*agree somewhat*	*neither agree nor disagree*	*disagree somewhat*	*strongly disagree*
European Union		36	5	6	1
Austria	5	22	5	7	1
Belgium	5	24	6	8	
Denmark	5	22	6	6	
Finland	5	18	5	4	
France	8	25	5	8	
Germany	8	26	8	8	1
Greece	4	14	5	6	1
Iceland	5	16	5	3	2
Ireland	6	19	4	7	1
Italy	4	19	7	6	1
Luxembourg	4	18	4	6	1
Netherlands	6	21	6	7	
Norway	5	22	6	6	
Portugal	5	17	4	7	1
Spain	6	17	7	7	1
Sweden	6	23	4	6	
Switzerland	6	25	3	7	2
Turkey	3	10	4	4	1
United Kingdom	11	27	6	7	
Europe	**107**	**385**	**100**	**120**	**13**
Canada	8	24	5	6	1
Mexico	3	12	2	3	2
United States	8	23	8	7	1
North America	**19**	**59**	**15**	**16**	**4**
Australia	5	20	7	8	1
Japan	3	16	6	4	2
New Zealand	5	14	6	7	1
Asia-Pacific	**13**	**50**	**19**	**19**	**4**
Brazil	2	8	1	2	4
China	1	4	4	4	3
India	1	2	2	2	2
Russia	2	8	6	2	3
TOTAL	**156**	**552**	**152**	**171**	**34**

Table 41

In countries where respondent trade association members already sell, testing and certification to satisfy conformity assessment requirements significantly increase costs

	strongly agree	agree somewhat	neither agree nor disagree	disagree somewhat	strongly disagree
European Union	2	4			
Austria	1	2			
Belgium	1	2			
Denmark	1	2			
Finland	1	2			
France	1	2			
Germany	1	2			
Greece	1	2			
Iceland	1	2			
Ireland	1	2			
Italy	1	2			
Luxembourg	1	2			
Netherlands	1	2			
Norway	1	3			
Portugal	1	2			
Spain	1	2			
Sweden	1	2			
Switzerland	1	3			
Turkey	1	3			
United Kingdom	1	2			
Europe	**19**	**41**			
Canada		5			
Mexico	1	3	2		
United States		6	1		
North America	**1**	**14**	**3**		
Australia	2	4			
Japan	1	3			
New Zealand	1	4	1		
Asia-Pacific	**4**	**11**	**1**		
Brazil		4	1		
China		3			
India		3			
Russia		4			
TOTAL	**26**	**84**	**5**	**0**	**0**

Table 42

In countries where respondent manufacturers already sell, testing and certification to satisfy conformity assessment requirements significantly reduce ability to get new products to market quickly

	strongly agree	agree somewhat	neither agree nor disagree	disagree somewhat	strongly disagree
European Union	11	19	7	13	7
Austria	3	15	5	10	4
Belgium	5	14	7	10	6
Denmark	4	15	7	8	3
Finland	4	11	4	7	3
France	7	16	6	8	7
Germany	10	16	4	12	6
Greece	3	9	4	8	4
Iceland	4	7	7	7	3
Ireland	3	12	6	9	4
Italy	4	11	6	8	6
Luxembourg	4	11	5	8	2
Netherlands	4	14	6	10	4
Norway	5	13	7	8	3
Portugal	4	11	6	8	4
Spain	3	14	6	10	4
Sweden	6	13	5	11	1
Switzerland	5	14	4	10	8
Turkey	2	8	4	6	2
United Kingdom	8	16	6	12	5
Europe	**88**	**240**	**105**	**170**	**79**
Canada	5	12	8	11	5
Mexico	3	6	2	6	3
United States	6	11	9	13	5
North America	**14**	**29**	**19**	**30**	**13**
Australia	3	8	10	11	5
Japan	2	7	8	7	4
New Zealand	3	6	8	7	4
Asia-Pacific	**8**	**21**	**26**	**25**	**13**
Brazil	1	4	2	3	5
China	1	4	2	5	3
India	1	3		2	2
Russia	2	2	7	3	5
TOTAL	**126**	**322**	**168**	**251**	**127**

Table 43

	strongly agree	agree somewhat	neither agree nor disagree	disagree somewhat	strongly disagree

In countries where respondent trade associations already sell, testing and certification to satisfy conformity assessment requirements significantly reduce ability to get new products to market quickly

	strongly agree	agree somewhat	neither agree nor disagree	disagree somewhat	strongly disagree
European Union		5		1	
Austria		3			
Belgium		3			
Denmark		3			
Finland		3			
France		3			
Germany		3			
Greece		3			
Iceland		3			
Ireland		3			
Italy		3			
Luxembourg		3			
Netherlands		3			
Norway		3		1	
Portugal		3			
Spain		3			
Sweden		3			
Switzerland		3		1	
Turkey		3		1	
United Kingdom		3			
Europe		**57**		**3**	
Canada	1	4			
Mexico	1	3	1		
United States	1	4	2		
North America	**3**	**11**	**3**		
Australia	1	3		1	
Japan		3			
New Zealand		3	1	1	
Asia-Pacific	**1**	**9**	**1**	**2**	
Brazil		3	1		
China		2			
India		2			
Russia		2		1	
TOTAL	**4**	**91**	**5**	**7**	**0**

Table 44

In countries where respondent manufacturers would like to sell, testing and certification to satisfy conformity assessment requirements would significantly increase costs

	strongly agree	agree somewhat	neither agree nor disagree	disagree somewhat	strongly disagree
European Union	2	2	2		1
Austria		1		1	1
Belgium		1			1
Denmark		4		1	1
Finland		2		3	2
France				1	1
Germany		2	1		1
Greece		3		1	2
Iceland		2	2	3	1
Ireland		4			1
Italy		1		3	1
Luxembourg		3			1
Netherlands		1			1
Norway		1	1	1	1
Portugal		1		1	1
Spain			1		2
Sweden		1		2	1
Switzerland		2		1	1
Turkey		5	2		2
United Kingdom			1	1	
Europe		**34**	**8**	**19**	**22**
Canada	3	2		2	
Mexico	2	2		2	
United States	4	1	1	1	1
North America	**9**	**5**	**1**	**5**	**1**
Australia	1	1		1	
Japan	1	3	2	1	
New Zealand	1	1	1	1	
Asia-Pacific	**3**	**5**	**3**	**3**	
Brazil	3	2		2	
China	1	6	1	1	
India	1	3	1	2	
Russia	4	2	1	3	
TOTAL	**23**	**59**	**17**	**35**	**24**

Table 45

In countries where respondent trade associations would like to sell, testing and certification to satisfy conformity assessment requirements would significantly increase costs

	strongly agree	agree somewhat	neither agree nor disagree	disagree somewhat	strongly disagree
European Union		1			
Austria					
Belgium					
Denmark					
Finland					
France					
Germany					
Greece					
Iceland					
Ireland					
Italy					
Luxembourg					
Netherlands					
Norway					
Portugal					
Spain					
Sweden					
Switzerland					
Turkey					
United Kingdom					
Europe					
Canada	1	1			
Mexico			1		
United States	1	1			
North America	**2**	**2**	**1**		
Australia		1			
Japan	2				
New Zealand		1			
Asia-Pacific	**2**	**2**			
Brazil			1		
China		2	1		1
India		1	1		1
Russia		2			1
TOTAL	**4**	**10**	**4**	**0**	**3**

Table 46

In countries where respondent manufacturers would like to sell, testing and certification to satisfy conformity assessment requirements significantly reduce ability to get new products to market quickly

	strongly agree	agree somewhat	neither agree nor disagree	disagree somewhat	strongly disagree
European Union	1	1	2	1	2
Austria			1	2	
Belgium			1	1	
Denmark		1		2	3
Finland		2		3	2
France				2	
Germany		2	1	1	
Greece		1		2	2
Iceland		2	2	3	1
Ireland		1	1	2	1
Italy		1		4	
Luxembourg		1	1	2	
Netherlands			1	1	
Norway			1	2	1
Portugal		1		2	
Spain			1	1	1
Sweden		2		2	
Switzerland		1	1	2	
Turkey		1	3	3	2
United Kingdom		2			
Europe		**18**	**14**	**37**	**13**
Canada	3	2		2	
Mexico	2	1	1	2	
United States	4	1	2		1
North America	**9**	**4**	**3**	**4**	**1**
Australia	1	2			
Japan	1	4	2		
New Zealand	1	2	1		
Asia-Pacific	**3**	**8**	**3**		
Brazil	3	1	1	2	
China	1	3	2	1	2
India	1	1	2	3	
Russia	3	2	1	3	1
TOTAL	**21**	**38**	**28**	**51**	**19**

Table 47

In countries where respondent trade associations would like to sell, testing and certification to satisfy conformity assessment requirements significantly reduce ability to get new products to market quickly

	strongly agree	agree somewhat	neither agree nor disagree	disagree somewhat	strongly disagree
European Union					
Austria					
Belgium					
Denmark					
Finland					
France					
Germany					
Greece					
Iceland					
Ireland					
Italy					
Luxembourg					
Netherlands					
Norway					
Portugal					
Spain	1				
Sweden					
Switzerland					
Turkey					
United Kingdom					
Europe	**1**				
Canada	1				
Mexico					
United States	1				
North America	**2**				
Australia					
Japan	1	1			
New Zealand					
Asia-Pacific	**1**	**1**			
China		1	1		1
India		1			1
Russia		1			1
TOTAL	**4**	**4**	**1**	**0**	**3**

Table 48 (Part 1)

Activities and location of respondent product safety and conformity assessment organisations: European countries

	Development of product safety standards	Promulgation or publication of standards	Accreditation of standards development organisations	Testing of products	Accreditation of product testing organisations	Certification of products	Accreditation of product certifying organisations	Registration of manufacturers' quality systems	Accreditation of quality systems registrars
European Union	15	5		11	1	16	1	8	
Austria	2	2		3		3		1	
Belgium				3		3		1	
Denmark	6	4		4	1	8	1	4	1
Finland	1			3	1	3	1		1
France				4		4		2	
Germany	2	1		5		4			
Greece	1	1		4		3			
Iceland				2		2		1	
Ireland				2		3		1	
Italy				4		3		1	
Luxembourg				2		2			
Netherlands				4		4		2	
Norway				2		2		1	
Portugal				3		3		1	
Spain				3		2		1	
Sweden	4	3		6	2	5	1	4	1
Switzerland				5		5		1	
Turkey				3		2		1	
United Kingdom	2			10	2	9	1	3	

Table 48 (Part 2)

Activities and location of respondent product safety and conformity assessment organisations: Non-European countries

	Development of product safety standards	Promulgation or publication of standards	Accreditation of standards development organisations	Testing of products	Accreditation of product testing organisations	Certification of products	Accreditation of product certifying organisations	Registration of manufacturers' quality systems	Accreditation of quality systems registrars
Canada	3	1		6	1	7	1	2	
Mexico	2	1		5	1	4	1	1	
United States	4	1		7	1	6	1	3	
Australia	4	3	2	6	1	5	1	1	
Japan	2	1		7	1	5	1	2	
New Zealand	1			5	1	4	1	1	
Brazil	1			4	1	3	1		
China	1			5	1	5	1		
India	1			3	1	3	1		
Russia	1			3	2	3	2		

Table 49

Responses by type of organisation

	# of responses	% of total responses
Government agency	5	12%
International or regional organisation	2	5%
Government-funded independent organisation	3	7%
Mixed government-private organisation	1	2%
Private non-profit organisation	19	46%
Private for-profit organisation	10	24%
Other	1	2%
TOTAL	**41**	**100%**

Note: Some respondents did not specify the type of organisation.

Table 50

Product standard and conformity assessment organisation responses by category

	# of responses	% of total responses
Toys	14	34%
Microwave Ovens	9	22%
Lawn Mowers	7	17%
Bicycle Helmets	11	27%
TOTAL	**41**	**100%**

Note: Some respondents did not specify the type of organisation.

Table 51

Product safety and conformity assessment organisation responses by country and region		
	# of responses	*% of total responses*
Austria	2	5%
Denmark	8	19%
Finland	2	5%
Germany	2	5%
Greece	1	2%
Sweden	6	14%
Switzerland	1	2%
United Kingdom	9	21%
Europe	**31**	**72%**
Canada	1	2%
Mexico	2	5%
United States	4	9%
North America	**7**	**16%**
Australia	4	9%
Japan	1	2%
Asia-Pacific	**5**	**12%**
TOTAL	**43**	**100%**

Table 52

Respondents' levels of involvement in development of product safety standards					
	strongly agree	*agree somewhat*	*neither agree nor disagree*	*disagree somewhat*	*strongly disagree*
The organisation's technical research played a significant role in the development of these standards.	11	9	3	3	8
Other already existing standards (industry/private sector; national; regional; or international) played a significant role in the development of these standards.	14	10	6	1	
Other already existing standards (industry/private sector; national; regional; or international) were wholly adopted as the organisation's standards.	6	2	3	7	15
The organisation promulgated or published these standards after they were developed by a related organisation.	11	1	2	2	15

Table 53

Factors that played a role in the development of product safety standards

	strongly agree	agree somewhat	neither agree nor disagree	disagree somewhat	strongly disagree
Consumer participation was significant in the development of these standards.	16	9	3	2	2
The participation of small- and medium-sized manufacturers played a significant role in the development of these standards.	9	9	7	6	1
The participation of the government (national, state or local) played a significant role in the development of these standards.	12	12	4	2	1
The participation of large manufacturers played a significant role in the development of these standards.	14	14		3	1
The participation of large trade associations played a significant role in the development of these standards.	12	7	6	3	4
The participation of foreign manufacturers or their representatives played a significant role in the development of these standards.	6	12	6	2	5
Serious consideration was given to international standards in the development of these standards.	13	7	3	3	2
Serious consideration was given to other regional, national or private-sector standards in the development of these standards.	5	11	9	2	1
Risk analysis showed that these product safety standards would significantly reduce the risk of injury.	9	8	9	2	2
The cost of conformity was a serious consideration in the development of these standards.	2	7	11	6	4
The benefits of injury reduction were balanced against the costs of conformance when developing these standards.	4	7	12	3	4

Table 54

Descriptive statements concerning particular product safety standards

	strongly agree	agree somewhat	neither agree nor disagree	disagree somewhat	strongly disagree
These product safety standards are significantly different from other product safety standards applicable to this product.	3	2	5	4	13
These product safety standards are similar to other product safety standards applicable to this product.	9	9	7	1	
These product safety standards reflect state of the art technology for this product.	11	12	5	1	
These product safety standards provide the same level of safety as other product safety standards applicable to this product.	8	4	9	2	2
These product safety standards provide a lower level of safety than other product safety standards applicable to this product.			5	4	17
Products manufactured to these product safety standards are safer than products manufactured to other product safety standards applicable to this product.	5	8	8	3	2
Products manufactured to these product safety standards will cost more than products manufactured to other product safety standards applicable to this product.	1	4	14	2	5
Products manufactured to these product safety standards will last longer than products manufactured to other product safety standards applicable to this product.		2	19	1	3
It is easier to manufacture products according to these safety standards than to manufacture them according to other product safety standards applicable to this product.	1		18	2	4

Table 55

Attitudes towards reducing differences among standards for particular products

	strongly agree	agree somewhat	neither agree nor disagree	disagree somewhat	strongly disagree
It would be difficult to develop an international product safety standard for this product because of a lack of interest among national and regional standards organisations.	3	1	4	7	16
It would be difficult to develop an international product safety standard for this product because of strong national differences regarding safety standards for this product.	5	6	6	7	7
Harmonisation of the various national and regional product safety standards applicable to this product is not necessary because the standards are basically equivalent.	6	4	10	5	6
Harmonisation of the various national and regional product safety standards applicable to this product would not be difficult because the standards are basically equivalent.	6	8	10	3	3
Harmonisation of the various national and regional product safety standards applicable to this product would be difficult because the standards are different.	3	1	6	12	7
Harmonisation of the various national and regional product safety standards applicable to this product would take too long.	1	6	7	8	7
Harmonisation of the various national and regional product safety standards applicable to this product would cost too much.	2	1	8	10	8
Harmonisation of the various national and regional product safety standards applicable to this product would be difficult because of rapid developments in product innovation.		2	8	6	13

Table 56

Opinions regarding the process for developing consumer product safety standards

	strongly agree	*agree somewhat*	*neither agree nor disagree*	*disagree somewhat*	*strongly disagree*
Consumer participation in the development of product safety standards is important.	23	7		1	1
The participation of small- and medium-sized manufacturers is important to the development of product safety standards.	16	14	2		
It is important that the product safety standard development process be open to foreign manufacturers and their trade associations.	14	7	6	4	1
The cost of conformance should be considered in the development of product safety standards.	9	9	9	3	2
The impact on trade is an important consideration in the development of product safety standards.	10	10	7	2	3
The impact on competition is an important consideration in the development of product safety standards.	7	9	7	5	3
Providing general notice of the development of product safety standards and an opportunity to comment during the development stage improves the final result.	24	5	3		
Serious consideration should be given to international standards in the development of product safety standards.	23	6	3		
Serious consideration should be given to other regional, national or private-sector standards in the development of product safety standards.	15	8	7	1	
Thorough risk analysis improves product safety standards.	19	11	1	1	
The benefits of injury reduction should be balanced against the costs of conformance when developing product safety standards.	10	7	6	5	3

Table 57

Reasons why product testing results might not be accepted in certain countries

	strongly agree	agree somewhat	neither agree nor disagree	disagree somewhat	strongly disagree
Foreign test results are not accepted for any consumer product as a matter of law.	2	2	1	1	2
Test results from the country where the respondent's organisation tests products are not accepted as a matter of law.	1	3	1	1	2
Foreign test results are not accepted as a matter of law.	1	3		2	2
Private certification programs for this product do not accept foreign test results.	3	3	1		2
Foreign product testing facilities cannot be accredited.	4	1	2		2
Foreign test results are generally accepted, but the respondent's organisation's facilities lack the required accreditation.		1		3	3
The respondent's organisation's product testing facilities lack the required accreditation because the accreditation process is too costly.			2	2	3
End consumers of this product demand testing by national bodies and will not accept foreign test results.	2	2	1	1	2
Distributors/importers demand testing by national bodies and will not accept foreign test results.	1	3	1	1	2
Local (i.e. sub-national) regulations are not satisfied by foreign test results.	2	3		2	1

Table 58

Reasons why product certification is not accepted in certain countries

	strongly agree	agree somewhat	neither agree nor disagree	disagree somewhat	strongly disagree
Foreign product certification not accepted for any consumer product as a matter of law.	1	1		2	2
Product certification from the country where the respondent's organisation certifies products is not accepted as a matter of law.		1		2	2
Foreign product certification is not accepted as a matter of law.		1		2	2
Foreign product certification is generally accepted, but the respondent organisation's facilities lack the required accreditation.		1		2	2
Foreign product certification programs cannot be accredited.	1		2		2
The respondent's organisation's product certification program/facility lacks the required accreditation because the accreditation process is too costly.				2	3
End consumers of this product demand testing by national bodies and will not accept foreign product accreditation.	1	2	1		2
Distributors/importers demand testing by national bodies and will not accept foreign product certification.	1	3			2
Local (i.e. sub-national) regulations are not satisfied by foreign product certification	3	1	1		1

Table 59

General statements concerning testing and certification

	strongly agree	agree somewhat	neither agree nor disagree	disagree somewhat	strongly disagree
For consumer product testing, re-testing a product according to different testing procedures rarely occurs.	6	5	4	4	3
For consumer product testing, significant additional costs are incurred when different national requirements make it necessary to re-test the same product to different testing procedures.	7	10	2	1	2
For consumer product testing, the respondent's organisation believes it should only be necessary to test a product once.	5	3	6	5	4
For consumer product testing, it is necessary for the respondent's organisation to have more than one accreditation of its testing facilities in order to serve clients who sell products internationally.	7	3	4	2	5
For consumer product testing, multiple accreditations of testing facilities from different accreditors do not improve the reliability of testing results.	12	5	2	1	
For consumer product testing, multiple accreditations of testing facilities from different accreditors increases costs significantly.	9	4	5	1	
For consumer product certification, national requirements for product certification are similar.	5	8	4	2	3
For consumer product certification, it is necessary for the respondent's organisation to have more than one accreditation in order to serve clients who sell internationally.	7	4	5	4	1
For consumer product certification, multiple accreditations of certification programs/facilities from different accreditors increases costs significantly.	6	8	5		
For consumer product certification, accredited certification programs should include consumer notification and recall provisions.	4	5	5	2	2

Annex 2

STANDARDISATION AND CONFORMITY ASSESSMENT IN THE EUROPEAN COMMUNITY

1. Background: The Treaty of Rome and the "Old Approach"

No single recent event has had more impact on the trade effects of product safety standardisation and conformity assessment than the regulatory approach of the European Community. It is therefore useful to briefly describe the key aspects of this approach, and their effects on product safety standards and conformity assessment.

The Treaty of Rome identified as one of the broad objectives the creation of a single market (Article 2). Article 30 of the Treaty specifically prohibits quantitative restrictions on imports and all other measures having equivalent effects. The only exception to this requirement is contained in Article 36, which allows Member States to take action which, among other reasons, could be justified on grounds of protecting health and human safety. Article 30 was interpreted by the European Court of Justice in the landmark "Cassis de Dijon" case in 1974, ruling that all products which have been produced and legally placed into commerce in one EU Member State must be admitted into all other EU Member States.

The ruling in "Cassis de Dijon" underscored the need to reduce the obstacles created by differing product requirements in establishing a single market. The first practical attempts to harmonise the differing technical regulations and standards were not always successful. The so-called "Old Approach" to technical harmonisation involved drafting detailed technical directives, and had limited success in establishing agreement on technical issues at a political level, largely because of a requirement for unanimous agreement among Member States. The effectiveness of the Old Approach was also limited due to its time-consuming procedures, and the perceived effects of the directives which were thought to stifle innovation and result in excessive uniformity. During this period, the number of new national regulations increased substantially while, at the same time, increasing attention was drawn to the difficulties created by the non-recognition of testing and certification processes between different Member States.

One significant exception to the Old Approach, and perhaps the most significant development in the area of standardisation before 1980, was the particular approach taken in 1973 in the provisions of the Low Voltage Directive (LVD). The approach taken in the LVD was different from other technical directives adopted at the time because it did not attempt to establish technically detailed product standards. Rather, the LVD contained references to product standards that could be followed to demonstrate that the product was safe and in compliance with the provisions of the LVD. The LVD was the first instrument of Community legislation involving references to European standards, and constituted a stepping-stone to what later was termed the "New Approach," described in Part 2 of this Annex.

By 1980, the need had become clear that a fairly bold approach would have to be adopted to address these issues. The first step in this direction was the adoption of Directive 83/189 establishing a procedure for the provision and exchange of information in the field of technical standards and regulations. The directive also mandated a waiting period during which the European Community could consider the need for a European initiative to be taken in response to a proposed national action and draw attention to possible barriers to trade. Despite making some progress in slowing the introduction of new national regulations, further action was still needed:

2.   The "New Approach" and Standardisation

The "New Approach" was introduced in 1985, and became a fundamental part of the 1992 Single Market program. The adoption of the New Approach was facilitated by co-operation agreements between European standards bodies and public authorities, and by the introduction in the European Council of weighted majority voting for directives concerning the establishment of the single market. The New Approach embodies the following four principles:

(a) Legislative harmonisation is limited to the adoption, by means of directives based on Article 100 of the EEC Treaty, of essential safety requirements (or other requirements in the general interest) with which products on the market must conform. Conforming products must be permitted free movement throughout the Community.

(b) The task of drawing up the technical standards needed for the production and placing on the market of products conforming to the essential requirements established by the directives is entrusted to organisations competent in the standardisation area.

(c) Technical standards are not mandatory and maintain their status of voluntary standards.

(d) National authorities are obliged to recognise that products manufactured in conformity with harmonised standards (or, provisionally, with national standards) are presumed to conform to the "essential requirements" established by the directive. The manufacturer has the choice of not manufacturing in conformity with the standards. In such an event, the manufacturer has an obligation to prove that its products conform to the essential requirements of the directive.

The New Approach hoped to achieve the following objectives: *(i)* easier adoption of directives because of changes to voting requirements and reduced technical content of the directives; *(ii)* removal of the European Commission from involvement in detailed technical standards by assigning the task to the European standards bodies; and *(iii)* concentration of product safety legislation on broader issues applicable to a range of product categories.

Final responsibility for the definition of product safety requirements, however, continues to rest with the European Community and not with standardisation bodies. The use of technical standards remains voluntary. The use of harmonised standards is promoted, however, with the presumption that any product manufactured in compliance with the appropriate European harmonised standard conforms with the requirements of the directive, unless the standards are shown to be inadequate.

Under the New Approach, the following product areas have been covered by specific directives: simple pressure vessels; toy safety; machinery; electromagnetic compatibility; non-automatic weighing machines; implantable medical equipment; medical devices; gas burning appliances; personal protective equipment; telecommunication equipment; construction products, explosives for civil use; hot water boilers; recreational craft; lifts; and equipment for use in potentially explosive atmospheres. In the future the number of New Approach directives will probably increase less rapidly. The Old Approach will most likely continue to be used for pharmaceuticals, pesticides, automobiles, chemicals, agricultural products and food additives.

With its direct reference to the use of European standards, the New Approach has had a significant impact on the standardisation sector, resulting in a large increase in the number of European standards projects. The number of such projects in the Comité européen de normalisation (CEN) alone has grown from approximately 2 000 in 1985 to over 8 000 today. At the national level, the proportion of activities associated with European or international standards has changed dramatically. In the early 1980s, for example, only ten per cent of the British Standards Institution's new national standards were European or international in origin. By 1995, that figure had grown to approximately 90 per cent.

Introduction of the New Approach Directives raised a number of concerns from non-EU parties that their reference to European standards could result in new technical barriers to trade. In practice, however, the introduction of European standards has enabled a corresponding reduction in differing national standards, and a higher degree of correlation with international standards developed in the ISO and IEC. The latter has been aided by co-operation agreements between the European and international standardisation bodies. The Vienna Agreement (1991) between CEN and the ISO ensures co-operation between the bodies through exchange of documents and information, the establishment of joint technical bodies, the transfer of standards projects for one organisation to the other and parallel voting on draft standards, so that a project developed at the international level can be adopted simultaneously as a European standard. CEN is also required under the Agreement to offer new standards projects to ISO before beginning such projects, and can only begin a project where there is lack of interest at the international level or because of serious time constraints. The Lugano Agreement (1990) ensures similar co-operation between CENELEC and the IEC. One result of this co-operation between the European and international standardisation bodies has been an increase in the extent to which European standards correspond to international ones: over 40 per cent of CEN standards, and as high as 90 per cent of CENELEC standards.

3. Conformity Assessment -- the "Global Approach"

Adoption of the New Approach led to a re-evaluation of conformity assessment issues. The Commission responded in 1989 by issuing a communication on a "Global Approach" to conformity assessment and testing, resulting in Council Resolution 90/C 10/01 of 21 December 1989. The Global Approach sought to complement the New Approach by creating new flexibility in the European certification system, and ensuring that conformity assessment procedures would not be used as barriers to trade.

The importance of a consistent approach to conformity testing within European legislation can be found in the following five fundamental principles embodied in the Global Approach, which recognised the need for:

(a) A pan-European testing and certification organisation that would promote non-regulatory mutual recognition agreements on testing and certification. Such an organisation should be flexible, serving as a forum within which mutual recognition agreements could be framed. The European Organisation for Testing and Certification (EOTC) was accordingly established in 1990.

(b) Common procedures for conformity assessment, as well as the criteria for the use of these procedures, and for the designation and notification of the competent bodies in each EU Member State. These procedures, termed "modules", were designed for the various phases of conformity assessment. The CE Mark would denote a claim of compliance with the relevant legislation, and allow free movement of such products within the Community.

(c) Promotion of European standards related to quality assurance (EN-29000 series which identify those quality system components that are needed to generate confidence in company capacity and efficiency in manufacturing products in line with pre-established requirements) and the encouragement to use accreditation (to the EN-45000 series which sets out the criteria to be met by accreditation, certification, testing and inspection bodies) when appointing notified bodies.

(d) Examination of the differing levels of development in testing and certification throughout the Community.

(e) Promotion of international trade in regulated products with non-EU countries. For mutual recognition agreements based on Article 113 of the EEC Treaty, the Community will ensure that the competence of such third countries is equivalent with their Community counterparts.

The different modules for the conformity assessment procedures applicable to products falling under New Approach directives were outlined in a 1990 Council Decision which was updated in 1993 (Council Decision 93/465/EEC of 22 July 1993). They are as follows: A - Internal check supported by manufacturer's self-declaration of conformance; B - EC-Type Examination; C - Conformity to type; D - Product QA EN-29002; E - Product QA EN-29003; F - Verification of Products; G - Verification on per-item basis; and H - Complete quality assurance EN-29001. Modules A, G and H refer to both design and manufacture, while Modules C, D, E and F refer to the manufacture of the product only and Module B to the design of the product only.

The actual choice of module is specified in the relevant New Approach directive, and reflects the perceived risk associated with the product, while allowing the manufacturer a margin of choice at the same time. For example, toys require in effect Module A (manufacturer's self-declaration of conformance) if the product conforms to a European harmonised standard. If the toy does not conform to European standards, Module B is required. The Gas Appliances Directive requires Module B (EC-type examination) in conjunction with other modules dealing with production. In the case of the Personal Protective Equipment Directive, products falling under its jurisdiction fall into three classes according to their relative risks where different procedures apply.

Where a module requires certification or testing by a third party, this must be carried out by a competent body. Testing and certification bodies must first be recognised as being competent by their national governments, and then notified to the Commission. These so-called "notified bodies" must be under the jurisdiction of the relevant national authority, meaning that EU Member States can only notify bodies established on their territory. A presumption of competence is given top those bodies which fulfil the EN-45000 standards requirements. The primary role of these notified bodies is to carry out, on behalf of public authorities and under their supervision, the conformity assessment procedures prescribed by the directives. Notified bodies are charged with carrying out their duties in a competent, transparent, neutral, independent and non-discriminatory manner. Mutual recognition of the work of notified bodies is meant to ensure acceptance of their compliance certificates throughout the Union and eliminate the need for re-testing. Notified bodies are permitted to do business throughout the European Union.

Successful application of the appropriate conformity assessment procedures outlined in the directives leads to the affixation of the CE marking onto the product. Affixation of the CE Mark of conformity is the final requirement before placing a product onto the market. Only products specifically covered by a New Approach directive can bear this symbol. The CE Mark is not primarily intended to inform consumers about the characteristics of a particular product, as in the case of a quality mark. Instead, the CE Mark is aimed at informing market inspection services and customs that the product is claimed to have been produced in conformity with the relevant New Approach directives. The appearance of the CE Mark on only certain consumer products as well the existence of other certification marks has contributed to some confusion on the part of consumers.

4.   Access to the European Market by Non-EU Manufacturers

Non-EU based manufacturers have two ways of having their products evaluated in non-EU countries in order to satisfy the third-party conformity assessment requirements of the New Approach directives. The first way is by means of a sub-contract arrangement between a notified body and a testing facility in a non-EU country. If such an agreement exists, the product can be tested at the testing facility in the non-EU country, but the tests must be evaluated and the product's compliance certified by the EU notified body. The sub-contracting body does not have to be notified to the EU, but must nonetheless be easily identifiable if required. The rules governing these arrangements are contained in the Commission "Guide to the Implementation of Community Harmonisation Directives Based on the New Approach and the Global Approach" (European Commission, Brussels, 1994), and require that sub-contracting testing bodies be qualified and competent. Testing bodies accredited in conformity with EN-45000 standards are presumed qualified.

The second way for non-EU manufacturers to have their products certified in non-EU countries depends on the existence of a mutual recognition agreement between the EU and the country where the certification takes place.   Such an agreement would delegate responsibility for certifying conformity to qualified certification organisations based in the non-EU country. The principles governing negotiations for such mutual recognition agreements are set forth in a mandate to the Commission in a Council Decision adopted on 21 September 1992, on the basis of which the Community is currently negotiating with a number of countries.

The Council Decision provides that the Commission may enter into mutual recognition agreements concerning product certification with non-EU countries if the following conditions are met: qualifying non-EU conformity assessment bodies must have equivalent levels of competence as their Community counterparts and maintain such levels; the subject matter of such agreements is limited to reports, certificates and marks drafted and issued directly by the qualified bodies; and the agreements must be balanced.

5. Relevance of the European Community model for OECD Member Countries

The standardisation and conformity assessment philosophy embodied in the New Approach and the Global Approach provide a useful model of how to regulate product safety effectively, in the least trade-restrictive manner possible, in conformity with the obligations of the WTO Agreement on Technical Barriers to Trade (TBT). The solutions chosen by the European Community may also be relevant for other regions or regional groupings seeking to establish a common regulatory approach while preserving heterogeneity and flexibility for industry and trade.

In the area of standards, significant reliance on international standards within the European Community creates economies of scale for suppliers of products to Community markets, while the possibility for different producers to rely on differing -- but functionally equivalent -- standards to achieve conformity to the essential health and safety requirements of the New Approach Directives provides significant flexibility to industry and to exporters to the European Community. This approach fulfils the obligation in the TBT Agreement to maintain standards as voluntary instruments, as well as the requirement to accept other parties' means of demonstrating conformity where these are equivalent.

In the area of conformity assessment, the Global Approach of the European Community seeks to achieve synergy between effective health and safety protection and the principle of least-trade restrictiveness. This is accomplished above all by the modular approach to conformity assessment through which producers are often given a choice of the means by which their product's conformity can be assessed. This, together with the adoption of different modular procedures according to the risk level of the sector or the product in question, offers an example of how to apply conformity assessment in a manner which gives flexibility, in proportion to the risks being assessed, according to the proportionality disciplines of the TBT Agreement. Reliance on Notified Bodies under the responsibility of the public authorities increases the flexibility open to producers seeking assessment of their products, and increases regulatory efficiency.

GLOSSARY OF ACRONYMS

A2LA American Association for Laboratory Accreditation

AFNOR Association Française de Normalisation (French Standards Institute)

ANEC European Association for the Co-ordination of Consumer Representation in Standardisation

ANSI American National Standards Institute

ANZCERTA Australia-New Zealand Closer Economic Relations Trading Agreement

APEC Asia-Pacific Economic Co-operation forum

ASEAN Association of South East Asian Nations

ASE Association Suisse des Electriciens (Swiss Electricians Association)

ASTM American Society for Testing and Materials

BEAMA Federation of British Electrotechnical and Allied Manufacturers' Association

BNM-FRETAC National Metrology Office (France)

BS British Standard

CASCO Conformity Assessment Policy Committee (ISO)

CB-FCS CB Full Certification Scheme of the IECEE

CCA CENELEC Certification Agreement

CE A mark indicating a declaration of conformity with the essential requirements in European Commission New Approach Directives

CEC Commission of the European Community

147

CECC CENELEC Electronic Components Committee

CEN Comité Européen de Normalisation (European Standards Institute)

CENELEC Comité Européen de Normalisation Electrotechnique (European Electrotechnical Standards Institute)

CEOC Confédération Européenne d'Organismes de Contrôle (European Confederation of Independent Inspecting Bodies)

CI Consumers International (formerly IOCU - the International Organisation of Consumers Unions)

COFRAC Comité Français d'Accréditation (French Accreditation Body)

COPOLCO Committee on Consumer Policy (ISO)

CPSC Consumer Product Safety Commission (United States)

CSA Canadian Standards Association

CSC Commission de la Sécurité des Consommateurs (French Consumer Safety Commission)

DABAK Danish national accreditation authority

DIN Deutsches Institut für Normung e.V. (German Standards Institute)

DGCCRF Direction générale de la concurrence, de la consommation et de la répression des fraudes (French Directorate-General for Competition, Consumer Affairs, and Fraud Repression)

DOF Diario official (Official Register, Mexico)

EAC European Accreditation for Certification

EAL European Co-operation for Accreditation of Laboratories

ECITC European Committee for IT Testing and Certification (EOTC Sectoral Committee)

ECOSA European Consumer Safety Association

EEA European Economic Area

EFTA European Free Trade Association

ELSECOM European Electrotechnical Sectoral Committee for testing and certification

EN European standard (Norme européene, Europäische Norm)

EOTC European Organisation for Testing and Certification

EPA Environmental Protection Agency (USA)

ESCIF European Committee for Intrusion and Fire Protection (EOTC Sectoral Committee)

EQS European Committee for Quality Assessment and Certification

ETSI European Telecommunications Standards Institute

EUROLAB European organisation of Testing and Analytical laboratories

EWSC European Water Sectoral Committee

FAA Federal Aviation Administration (United States)

FAO Food and Agriculture Organisation (United Nations)

FCC Federal Communications Commission (United States)

FDA Food and Drug Administration (USA)

FINAS Finnish national accreditation authority

FTA Foreign Trade Association

GATT General Agreement on Tariffs and Trade

GIFAM Groupement interprofessionnel des fabricants d'appareils d'équipement ménager (French Professional Association of Manufacturers of Household Appliances)

GLP Good Laboratory Practice

GMP Good Manufacturing Practice

GS Geprüfte Sicherheit mark (German safety mark)

IAF International Accreditation Forum

IEC International Electrotechnical Commission

IECEE IEC System for Conformity Testing to Standards for Safety of Electrical Equipment

IECQ International Electrotechnical Commission Quality Assessment System for Electronic Components

IEP Electrotechnical Institute (Portugal)

IIOC Independent International Organisation for Certification

ILAC International Laboratory Accreditation Conference

IPQ Portuguese Quality Institute

ISO International Organisation for Standardisation

ISONET ISO Information Network

IQCL Industrial Quality Control Laboratory (Portugal)

ITU International Telecommunication Union

IWQ Institute of Welding and Quality (Portugal)

LMBG Law on Foodstuffs and Utility Goods (Germany)

LNE Laboratoire National d'Essais (French National Testing Laboratory)

LUM Voluntary Standardisation Agreement Scheme for Lighting Fixtures

LVD Low Voltage Directive (European Commission)

MD Machine Directive (European Commission)

MERCOSUR Mercado Común del Sur (South American Common Market)

MITI Ministry of International Trade and Industry (Japan)

MOU Memorandum of Understanding

MRA Mutual Recognition Agreement

NAFTA North American Free Trade Agreement

NCAP New Car Assessment Program (United States)

NED Noise Emissions Directive (European Commission)

NEMKO Private independent testing and certification body for electrotechnology (Norway)

NF Marque française de normalisation (French standardisation mark)

NISU National Injury Surveillance Unit (Australia)

NOM Norma Official Mexicana (Mexico)

ORGALIME Organisme de Liaison des Industries Métalliques Européennes (European Liaison Organisation for Metal Industries)

PPE Personal Protection Equipment (the subject of Directive 89/686/EEC of the European Commission)

QSAR Quality System Assessment Recognition Program (ISO/IEC)

RNE Réseau national d'essais (former French Accreditation Body for laboratories, now included in COFRAC)

SECOFI Mexican national accreditation authority

SEMKO Private testing, certification and inspection company for electrotechnology (Sweden)

SME small- and medium-sized enterprise

ST Toy Safety Standard (Japan)

SWEDAC Swedish Board for Accreditation and Conformity Assessment

TBT Technical Barriers to Trade Agreement (WTO)

TICQA Testing Inspection Calibration and Quality Assurance database (EOTC)

TS Turkish Standards Institute mark of conformity to safety standards

TÜV Technisches Überwachungsverein, an independent testing laboratory based in Germany

UKAS United Kingdom national accreditation authority

UL Underwriters Laboratories (United States)

VDE Verband Deutscher Elektrotechniker e.V. (Association of German Electrical Engineers)

WHO World Health Organisation

WTO World Trade Organisation

WWW World Wide Web

Notes

---

[1] This has been accompanied by the introduction of strengthened product liability legislation and, where relevant, frequent sizeable jury awards to victims of injuries caused by defective products.

[2] This report recognises that "mutual recognition" or "MRA" in this context is a generic term subject to different technical interpretations. For example, mutual recognition of conformity assessment may take the following forms:

(i) Government to government agreements. In this case, Government A will accept certificates from a certifying body in Country B as evidence that A's legal requirements have been satisfied. These types of agreements indicate that bodies are recognised as both competent and knowledgeable. Agreements of this type are currently being negotiated between the European Union and some non-EU countries. This is described in greater detail in Annex 2.

(ii) Agreements between accreditation bodies. Here, conformity assessment bodies in Country A are accredited by A's accreditation body, and conformity assessment bodies in Country B are accredited by B's accreditation body, and the two accreditation bodies agree among themselves that the criteria they apply are broadly the same (e.g. ISO 45000) and therefore the competence of the accredited conformity assessment bodies in A and B is broadly the same, and their results are reciprocally recognised.

(iii) Agreements between certifying bodies. For example, conformity assessment body X has such confidence in conformity assessment body Y that it will take responsibility for awarding its own certificate on the basis of Y's testing and certification with little or no further testing.

(iv) Mutual recognition enforced in legislation, as in Treaty of Rome sec. 36.

Types i and iv refer to agreements in the regulatory sector, and ii and iii to market-based or voluntary agreements. This report refers to all four different types of mutual recognition at various times, and the precise meaning must be inferred from the context.

[3] The questionnaire was sent to 23 Member countries. Seventeen Member countries responded including Australia, Austria, Belgium, Canada, Denmark, Finland, France, Germany, Japan, Mexico, the Netherlands, Portugal, Sweden, Switzerland, Turkey, the United Kingdom and the United States.

[4] For example, the system in Turkey is controlled by the Turkish Standards Institute, and in Australia the system is formed by a mix of federal, state and territorial agencies, and private institutions.

[5] Australian toy standards are subject to national standards which are equivalent to US standards. In Japan, Mexico and Turkey, toys are subject to national standards. Japanese toy standards are equivalent to those published by ISO and CEN. Mexican toy standards are equivalent to ISO and ASTM standards, while official Mexican standards are equivalent to IEC standards. In Switzerland, toys are dealt with in the Food and General Merchandise Act. The regulations are currently being revised and are largely based on EC Directive 88/378/EEC. The new regulation, which will probably come into force in 1995, contains "essential requirements" and refers to CEN standards. Turkish toy standards are equivalent to international standards. The United States has a number of federal toy regulations issued by the Consumer Product Safety Commission (CPSC) as well as voluntary toy standards published by private standards organisations, such as ANSI and ASTM.

[6] Denmark, Finland, and Japan are currently working on revisions to their toy standards.

[7] While two European countries responded that their toy standards are voluntary (France and Sweden), four others indicated that the same standards were mandatory (Austria, Belgium, Denmark and Portugal). The Finnish Decree on Toy Safety makes the CEN standards mandatory in Finland. In the future, however, these Finnish standards will become voluntary. Toy standards in Australia, Japan, Mexico, Turkey and the United States are a mix of mandatory and voluntary standards.

[8] Australian and Turkish toy standards are performance based, Japanese toy standards are design-based, Mexican toy standards are both design and performance standards, and US mandatory and voluntary toy standards contain performance requirements, although some have design requirements.

[9] All microwave oven standards in Austria, Denmark, Finland and Switzerland have been incorporated into mandatory regulations which refer to the relevant standards. Microwave oven standards in Belgium, the Netherlands and Portugal are design standards, while Germany, Sweden, the United Kingdom and the United States have performance standards. This characterisation may reflect lack of clarity in individual countries about the precise definition of "performance" or "design" standards. The safety standards of CENELEC countries are in principle identical with the European standard EN 60335-2-25 (individual countries may have different national numberings or designations). Yet some CENELEC countries report that this standard is a design standard, and others report that it is a performance standard. Japanese microwave ovens must conform to mandatory standards under the Electric Appliance and Material Control Law. Standards for Japanese microwave ovens are equivalent to IEC standards. Japanese microwave oven standards are design-based, and the institution involved in the development of microwave oven standards is MITI. Mexican microwave standards are both design and performance standards, and the institution involved in development is the General Standards Office of the Ministry of Trade. Official Mexican standards for microwave ovens are mandatory. In the United States, voluntary microwave ovens standards were developed and published by Underwriters Laboratories (UL)

(Standard 923) and were also published as an ANSI/UL standard (923-1991). The standards have been revised frequently and are currently again undergoing revision. Microwave ovens in the United States must also comply with federal regulations regarding microwave radio frequency standards issued by the US Food and Drug Administration. The State of Maryland, however, requires that microwave ovens sold in its jurisdiction conform with the applicable voluntary standards developed by UL.

[10] The Low Voltage Directive was promulgated by the European Community in 1973 and has since been revised.

[11] The "Old Approach" and "New Approach" are described in detail in Annex 2: Standardisation and Conformity Assessment in the European Community.

[12] The Noise Emissions Directive was promulgated in 1984, and has been revised several times since. The Machine Directive was promulgated in 1989.

[13] The Netherlands Standardisation Institute and the Sveriges Mekanstandardisering Organisation in Sweden were involved in developing the CEN technical standards for petrol-driven lawn mowers.

[14] Electric lawn mower standards in Japan were developed in 1962 by MITI. Japanese lawn mowers must conform to design-based mandatory standards under the Electric Appliance and Material Control Law (which also applies to microwave ovens). The Japanese lawn mower standards are equivalent to IEC standards. In Mexico, electric lawn mowers are subject to both mandatory and voluntary standards. The Mexican mandatory standards for electric lawn mowers are set forth in NOM 001-SCFI-1993 and are equivalent to the international standards set out in IEC-65-1985. Official Mexican Standard NOM-003-SCFI-1993 applicable to lawn mowers came into effect in 1993, and was developed with the involvement of many government agencies and private institutions. The Mexican voluntary standard NMX-J74-1982 was developed by a private firm and by the Ministry of Natural Resources and Industrial Development. In Sweden, it appears that other standards also apply to petrol-driven lawn mowers, in particular, ISO-5395:1990 (Power lawn and garden equipment). Switzerland indicated that lawn mowers are regulated in the Act on Safety of Technical Appliances. The regulation is currently under revision. Petrol-driven lawn mowers in Turkey are subject to Turkish Standards Institute standards TS-4937, developed in 1986, and TS-7419, developed in 1989. They are voluntary performance standards and are equivalent to ISO-5395 standards. Neither standard has been modified. In the United Kingdom, British Standard BS 5107:1974 is equivalent to the ISO standard. The United States applies mandatory standards to petrol-driven lawn mowers, and voluntary standard ANSI B71.1 "Safety Specifications for Walk-Behind and Ride-on Machines with Mowers" applies to "walk-behind" and "riding" lawn mowers. In addition, there are mandatory standards for walk-behind petrol-driven lawn mowers codified at 16 CFR 1205. The ANSI voluntary standard for lawn mowers was first developed in the 1960s and has since been modified many times. The ANSI riding mower standards are currently under revision. The CPSC mandatory standard was first developed in the 1970s and became effective in 1982. The ISO standards for power lawn and garden equipment were developed in the late 1970s.

15   In Australia, bicycle helmet standards are set forth in Australian Standard (AS 2063.2-1990). It is a mandatory performance standard. Japan's bicycle helmet standards are voluntary and were developed by the Consumer Product Safety Association. The Japanese bicycle helmet standards contain both design and performance standards. Mexico is currently revising existing Official Mexican Standard NOM-S-17-1978 to make it apply more generally to personal protective equipment of different types. Originally NOM-S-17-1978 applied only to helmets used with motorcycles. The new standard will be mandatory and will contain both performance and design elements. The Personal Protective Equipment (PPE) Directive came into effect in Finland and in Sweden in July 1995. Before the PPE went into effect in Sweden, bicycle helmet guidelines existed and contained performance standards based on the so-called "SP-method". In the United Kingdom, British Standard BS 6863:1989 is a voluntary standard currently applicable to bicycle helmets, but it will be withdrawn when the CEN standard becomes effective. The situation in the United States is in transition. Since March 1995, the law requires that bicycle helmets sold in the United States conform to at least one of several voluntary standards, on an interim basis, until the CPSC develops a mandatory bicycle helmet standard. The interim standards are those developed by the American National Standards Institute (ANSI) (Z90.4-1984), ASTM (F1447-94 or F1446-93), SNELL Memorial Foundation (B-90, B-90S, N-94 and B-95) and the Canadian Standards Association (CAN/CSA-D113.2-M89). They are all performance standards.

16   The Australian standards are based on American (ANSI Z90.4 and SNELL and New Zealand bicycle standards (NZS 5439). In Australia, bicycle helmet standards were developed under the auspices of the Standards Association of Australia by federal and state consumer affairs agencies, road traffic authorities, helmet manufacturers and testing authorities. The standards were first promulgated in 1988 and have been updated twice, most recently in 1992. Bicycle helmet standards in Japan were developed in 1983 by the Consumer Product Safety Association and have not been modified since. The Mexican draft standards refer to American (ANSI Z89.11969) and Canadian standards (CAN/CSA-Z94.1-92). In Mexico, revisions to NOM-S-1978 are being drafted by several ministries and private sector firms. In Switzerland, the Technical Appliances Act which is currently being revised will establish a "reference to standards" provision. The standard currently used is based on a US standard and on an EU regulation for motorcycle helmets. The PPE Directive was promulgated by the European Commission in 1989. Work on the CEN standard for bicycle helmets is being undertaken by national standards organisations. In the United States, the voluntary standards for bicycle helmets were first developed in 1973 by SNELL and have undergone several revisions.

17   The PPE Directive was promulgated by the European Community in 1989.

18   In Japan, there are criminal penalties for marketing toys, microwave ovens and lawn mowers which fail to conform with legal technical standards. In Mexico, the full range of civil and criminal penalties are available to the authorities to enforce mandatory standards, including product warnings, recalls, fines, closure of the business establishment, revocation of accreditation and administrative arrest. In Portugal, microwave ovens that do not conform to the applicable standard may face confiscation by regional delegations of the Ministry of Industry, but no official penalties have been developed. In Sweden, failure to conform with the LVD means that the microwave oven cannot be sold. If a non-conforming microwave oven is sold, the Swedish authorities can seek an injunction and penalties.

19   Conformity with either a mandatory or voluntary standard is not an absolute defence in product liability lawsuits in the United States, however.

20   The Labour Safety Act and the Product Safety Act also apply to non-conforming lawn mowers in Finland. The US mandatory standard for lawn mowers is enforced by the CPSC which can seek various civil and criminal penalties. Non-conforming lawn mowers cannot be imported into the United States and are subject to an order for repair, replacement or repurchase. The CPSC cannot, however, enforce US voluntary standards, which poses certain problems since it is possible that non-conformance with a voluntary safety standard may cause a defect creating a substantial risk of injury. In such a case, the general product safety law (the Consumer Product Safety Act) would give the CPSC authority to address the risk of injury.

21   Belgian officials rely on the Product Safety Act in assessing safety risks associated with bicycle helmets, in addition to the PPE Directive. Safety helmets sold in Finland are still subject to the Product Safety Act. In Finland and Sweden, there were no consequences for failing to conform to the PPE until July 1995. Japan does not provide for any legal consequences for marketing bicycle helmets which do not conform to bicycle helmet standards. The proposed standards in Mexico are not yet in effect, but when they are promulgated, enforcement authorities will have available to them the same options that are available for enforcing conformity assessment requirements applicable to other product categories such as toys and microwave ovens. In the United States, conformance to one of the four voluntary standards is required, and failure to conform to one of the standards can subject the product to recall and/or other civil or criminal penalties.

22   Australia, Belgium, Denmark, Germany, Finland, France, Japan, Sweden, the United Kingdom and the United States currently allow manufacturer's self-declaration of conformance for most of the products surveyed. Manufacturers self-declaration is an option in Switzerland. Manufacturer's self-declaration of conformance is not allowed in Mexico.

23   Technical files must be available for all products conforming to European Community Directives.

24   Finland requires testing of lawn mowers for conformance to the Noise Emissions Directive by the Technical Research Centre of Finland, the Manufacturing Technology or Safety Engineering and will also accept testing from other notified bodies. In Japan, testing and certification is prescribed by the Electrical Appliance and Material Control Law which requires that both domestic and foreign manufacturers of lawn mowers and microwave ovens sold in Japan be registered with MITI. Type approval must be received from MITI for microwave ovens and lawn mowers. Certification is voluntary in the Netherlands. In Mexico, in order to sell any of the four products, a certificate must be obtained from the General Standards Office, but there are no conformity assessment requirements with respect to voluntary lawn mower standards. Portugal requires third-party testing. In Switzerland, certification by the competent national testing body, the Association Suisse des Electriciens (ASE), is mandatory before placing microwave ovens on the market, while type approval for microwave ovens is not mandatory. There are no conformity assessment requirements for lawn mowers in Turkey. Third-party certification for microwave ovens is voluntary in the United

States, and it is the common practice. Organisations which certify microwave ovens and lawn mowers include UL, the CSA and ETL Testing Laboratories. There is no government accrediting organisation for these institutions. Qualifications are generally supported by the recognition and reputation in the market (including insurance companies, consumers, retailers and local jurisdictions) of the competence of the testing or certifying organisation. The conformity assessment system in the United States is made up of private organisations. In the United States, certification requirements for lawn mowers only exist for the mandatory standard which is set out in 16 CFR 1205.30-36. The United States does not have any requirements for testing and certifying organisations, and foreign conformity assessment results are accepted.

25   France has several bodies that have been accredited by the Ministry of Industry as competent to certify bicycle helmets as conforming to the PPE Directive. In the Netherlands, there is one notified body competent to conduct EC-type testing for bicycle helmets. In Sweden, the Swedish National Testing and Research Institute is accredited to test and certify bicycle helmets. Although Finland has no conformity assessment requirements for bicycle helmets manufacturers, its safety authorities have requested that the Swedish National Testing and Research Institute test bicycle helmets sold in Finland because there are no accredited institutions to test and certify bicycle helmets in Finland. Since July 1995, Sweden and Finland only accept test results from bodies accredited according to the requirements of the PPE. In Australia, there are no national conformity assessment requirements under the Federal Trade Practices Act; however, certain states require certification to the standard by the Standards Association of Australia. In Japan, testing and certification is prescribed by the Electrical Appliance and Material Control Law which requires that both domestic and foreign manufacturers of lawn mowers and microwave ovens sold in Japan be registered with MITI. Type approval must be received from MITI for microwave ovens and lawn mowers. In Japan, the conformity assessment requirements associated with the voluntary standard for personal protective equipment are managed by the Consumer Product Safety Association. The Consumer Product Safety Association allows domestic and foreign manufacturers of bicycle helmets to satisfy conformity assessment requirements either by "lot approval" or by "factory registration and model approval." Testing requirements for either type of approval may be done by foreign testing bodies designated by the Consumer Safety Association. Once helmet standards go into effect in Mexico, it will be necessary to obtain a certificate from the General Standards Office in order to market bicycle helmets. In the United States, manufacturer's self-declaration of conformance is the general rule for bicycle helmets. Testing and certification to the SNELL standards is done by SNELL for those who wish to use the SNELL label.

26   The notified bodies are normally notified by the relevant ministries of the member states, e.g. in Belgium by the Ministry of Economic Affairs and in France by the Ministry of Industry. In Sweden the notification and assessment is carried out by the accreditation body SWEDAC, which is also the central governmental authority for issues related to conformity assessment. National accreditation authorities include DABAK in Denmark, FINAS in Finland, UKAS in the United Kingdom and the Portuguese Quality Institute (IPQ) in Portugal.

27   Denmark and the Netherlands have two notified bodies in each of their countries that are competent to do EC-type testing for toys. In the United Kingdom, the institutions involved are largely private testing laboratories, although some are operated by local authorities.

28   Testing and certification bodies must conform to the EN-45000 series of standards in Belgium, Denmark, France, Portugal, Sweden. In the Netherlands, the Dutch Council for Certification, which designates testing bodies, encourages conformance with the EN-45000 series of standards but does not require such conformance. The United Kingdom takes the same position as the Netherlands.

29   The United Kingdom accepts notified results from Notified Bodies and from testing organisations endorsed by Notified Bodies. The United Kingdom also indicated that conformity assessment results from outside of Europe not endorsed by a Notified Body would be given due consideration.

30   Testing and certification results from any European notified body are generally accepted in other EU countries. The Dutch Delegate indicated that its notified bodies may accept test results from non-EU countries when they conform to certain standards (EN-45000). There are no restrictions on foreign testing or certification in the United States.

31   Denmark, Finland, Portugal, Sweden, and Switzerland in many cases accept conformity assessment results from organisations that are members of the CB certification system of the IECEE and the CCA certification system of CENELEC. Finland also accepts testing and certification results from those participating in the Nordic Certification System. The European Association for the Accreditation of Laboratories (EAL) and the European Accreditation for Certification (EAC) have entered into agreements with Australia and New Zealand to accept each other's testing and certification results. Japan is part of the IECEE-CB system and the conditions required by MITI for acceptance of foreign testing and certification are based on that system. In Japan, conformity testing to mandatory standards is done by testing bodies designated by MITI. Testing to voluntary standards is done by testing bodies designated by the Japan Toy Association. With respect to mandatory standards, Japan will accept foreign testing and certification results if they meet requirements established by MITI, for voluntary toy standards, but Japan will generally not accept foreign testing and certification results. MITI is also the national accrediting organisation. Manufacturer's self-declaration of conformance is not allowed in Japan. The exceptions to this practice include Korean and Hong Kong manufacturers. In Mexico, for all product categories, the national accrediting organisation (SECOFI) and private certifying bodies perform conformity assessment requirements. Mexico will accept foreign testing and certification results if a mutual recognition agreement exists with SECOFI. In Switzerland, the new draft regulations do not include any testing or certification requirements. In Turkey, testing is conducted by the Turkish Standards Institute which is also the national standards and accrediting organisation. Turkey will accept foreign testing and certification results from organisations with whom it has mutual recognition agreements.

32   Widespread confusion surrounding the actual meaning of the CE mark is discussed in Annex 2: Standardisation and Conformity Assessment in the European Community.

33   In the European Union, the marketing of lawn mowers that fail to conform to the Machine Directive or bicycle helmets that fail to conform to the conformity assessment requirements of the PPE Directive is illegal and can result in criminal penalties. In addition, lawn mowers are

subject to the Product Safety Directive. Failure to conform to testing and certification requirements in Denmark and Belgium could result in legal penalties. In Sweden, such sanctions will be pursued if non-conformance creates a risk of injury. Finland and Portugal are authorised to confiscate or ban non-conforming products, but they are not authorised to penalise the responsible party. In Japan, failure to follow the conformity assessment requirements for microwave ovens will result in the product being prohibited from the market and may result in criminal penalties. Failure to follow the conformity assessment requirements of the Consumer Product Safety Association for bicycle helmets or of the Toy Association for toys may result in the product being prohibited from bearing the respective mark. Consumers who are injured as a result of a defective safety helmet bearing the SG mark can be compensated for damages up to ¥ 30 million per person. The sanctions in Mexico for failure to abide by testing and certification requirements are the same as those for failure to conform to mandatory standards. They include fines, closure of the business, suspension or revocation of the license, product recalls and administrative arrest. In Turkey, the available sanctions include cancellation of the conformity certificate issued by the Turkish Standards Institute. Testing and certification procedures in the United States are a private matter between the manufacturer and the testing and certifying organisation and therefore, any dispute would be a civil matter between the parties. Conformity assessment requirements for mandatory standards in the United States are enforced by a number of civil and criminal penalties. Once the proposed mandatory standard for bicycle helmets goes into effect in the United States, failure to adhere to the certification and record keeping requirements will subject firms to civil and/or criminal penalties.

34   In France, while not required, manufacturers are encouraged to conform to ISO 9000 standards. Manufacturers must be registered with MITI in Japan. Registration is an option in Mexico and conformance to standards similar to the ISO 9000 series of standards forms a part of its certification system. Forty foreign firms in Mexico have been granted ISO 9000 certification by ISO accredited organisations. The Mexican conformity assessment system is undergoing reforms which would result in a larger role for the market in assuring the qualifications of testing and certification organisations. In the Netherlands, the Dutch Council for Certification often registers accrediting organisations and will accept foreign registration in certain cases. In Sweden, SWEDAC will enter into agreements with foreign organisations regarding the acceptance of foreign registrations. In Turkey, the Turkish Standards Institute registers systems and enters into mutual recognition agreements to accept foreign registrations; Turkey has already entered into mutual recognition and co-operation agreements with approximately 25 countries. In the United Kingdom, UKAS controls the ISO 9000 registration bodies. In the United States, private-sector certifiers are working with foreign organisations on product safety certification programs which may lead to greater acceptance of foreign conformity assessment results.

35   Toy manufacturers in particular responded that toys conform to EN-71 and EN-50082 in the European Union; in Japan, the Japanese sanitation law and toy safety standard; in the United States, US Federal Regulations, 16 CFR 1500, ASTM F963, ASTM F834 and ANSI Z315; and in Canada, Canadian toy standards. The safety standards applicable to microwave ovens include: the Low Voltage Directive 73/23/EEC; EN 60335-2-25; the Japanese Electrical Appliance Law; ANSI/UL 923-1981; US Federal regulations 21 CFR 1030; and IEC 335-2-25. According to lawn mower manufacturers in the European Union, the New Approach stipulates

that electric lawn mowers must conform to the LVD 73/23/EEC. All lawn mowers (petrol-driven as well as electric) must meet the requirements of the Machine Directive 89/392/EEC and the Noise Emissions Directive 84/538/EEC (as amended by 87/252/EEC, 88/180/EEC and 88/181/EEC) and must conform to the draft CEN standard for lawn mowers (pr EN 836). German lawn mower manufacturers responded that their lawn mowers must conform to the German DIN 1856/1858 standards. Manufacturers in the United Kingdom indicated that their lawn mowers conform to British standards BS 5107 and BS 3456. Lawn mowers sold in the United States must conform to the standards set forth in 16 CFR 1205 and ANSI B71.1. Several manufacturers indicated that their lawn mowers meet the international standard for lawn mowers ISO-5395:1990 (Power lawn and garden equipment). The bicycle helmets produced by respondents conform to a variety of bicycle helmet safety standards including the CE essential requirements set forth in the PPE Directive; in Germany the TÜV, GS and E-DIN 33954 (02/91); in the United Kingdom the BSI standards; and in the United States ANSI Z90.4-1984, ASTM F1446-7 or SNELL B-90 (B-90S, N-94 or B-95).

36   Both toy and lawn mower manufacturers indicated their desire for the elimination of differences among the various safety standards. In particular, toy manufacturers favour the harmonisation of CEN and ASTM standards, while lawn mower manufacturers mentioned harmonisation of the CEN and ANSI standards. Some toy manufacturers indicated that the Japanese toy safety standard should be harmonised with European and American standards. Most American and some European manufacturers focused on the CEN standards and cited the need to base such safety standards on scientific data and accepted risk analysis procedures. Lawn mower manufacturers indicated approval of the draft CEN standard, but criticised the time it has taken to be developed. American lawn mower manufacturers specifically criticised the CEN standards development process from which they were excluded and expressed concern about particular provisions in the draft standard and the justification of those provisions. Several Japanese respondents expressed concern about the provisions of the EU Machine Directive and expressed the view that it needed to be clarified. Some respondents did not like the idea of improving the standards because they believed that any changes would result in increased costs. Japanese and European microwave oven manufacturers focused their comments largely on UL standards. North American manufacturers commented on the CEN standards. Most of the comments had specific procedural and substantive suggestions regarding particular provisions in the UL and CEN standards. Other comments were more general, such as the need to harmonise the UL standard with the international standards (IEC 335-2-25), and the suggestion to have the Canadian standard adopt the UL standard as its own.

37   Twelve manufacturers responded that they had participated in the development of the EN-71 standard, at a cost of between US$ 10 000 and US$ 50 000. Responding toy manufacturers mentioned that they had participated in the development of the ASTM, CEN and Japanese toy safety standards. The costs of participation varied from "several thousand dollars" to over US$ 1 million for one large toy trade association. Lawn mower manufacturers responded that they had participated in the development of the GS standard, pr EN-836, pr EN-774, IEC 335-2-77 and ANSI B 71.1. The cost of participation ranged from US$ 5 000 to US$ 10 000 for lawn mower manufacturers to "tens of thousands of dollars" for one lawn mower trade association. Microwave oven respondents indicated that they had worked on the development of CEN, UL, IEC and Japanese standards. One bicycle helmet manufacturer responded that it

had participated in the development of the ASTM standard at a cost of approximately US$ 2 000.

[38] A number of toy respondents cited not being allowed to participate in the CEN standards development process. In particular, responses from American toy manufacturers focused on their exclusion from the CEN standardisation process. One toy manufacturer respondent indicated that his firm was not allowed to participate in the development of the ASTM standard. Lawn mower manufacturers had not participated in the development of pr EN 836, ANSI B 71.1, ISO 5395, BS EN 292/294 and the Machine Directive (89/392/EEC). Microwave oven respondents mentioned not having participated in the development of the UL standard, the CEN standard and the Australian standard. Bicycle helmet respondents mentioned the TÜV, DIN, CEN and SNELL standards. With respect to the DIN standard, one respondent indicated that his firm was not permitted to participate in the process. The respondents who identified the CEN standards indicated that it was a matter of priorities and that they thought that they could live with the result. The respondent who identified the SNELL standard indicated not being permitted to participate in the process and dissatisfaction with the standards development procedures.

[39] According to toy manufacturers, the most common testing and certification method is by government designated bodies, particularly in Europe and Japan. For those lawn mower manufacturers who identified Europe, the most frequently cited testing and certification method is a manufacturer's self-declaration of conformance and testing and certification by a government designated body. For those lawn mower manufacturers whose most important market is the United States, a manufacturer's self-declaration of conformance is the most commonly cited form of conformity assessment. The markets identified by microwave oven manufacturers were the European Union, Japan and the United States. The most frequently cited testing and certification method is by non-government bodies. The second most common method is the manufacturer's declaration of conformity. The markets identified by bicycle helmet manufacturers were the European Union and the United States. The most frequently cited testing and certification method is by government designated bodies in Europe.

[40] This provides further evidence of confusion and misunderstandings about the meaning of various marks, even in the manufacturing community. The GS mark, for example, is a pure safety mark, and has no quality associations.

[41] Toy manufacturers identified the CE, the ST (the Japanese toy safety standard) and the Lion markings. A majority of toy manufacturers and trade associations responded that consumers believe erroneously that these certification marks mean that the product is safe, that the product meets high quality standards and government safety standards. Responding lawn mower manufacturers indicated that lawn mowers may bear several certification including the CE, the OPEI, the GS and the BS marks. With respect to the OPEI, the BS and the GS marks, manufacturers and trade associations are generally of the view that the consumers think these marks indicate that the product is safe and that it meets high quality standards of a respected body. Responding microwave oven manufacturers identified the Dentori, GS, NF, S, UL and VDE marks. Respondents indicated that consumers understand the Dentori mark to mean that the product meets government standards and that the S mark means that the product meets the standards of a respected institution. With respect to the NF mark, respondents indicated that

consumers understand it to mean that the product meets government standards, that it is permitted to be sold on markets and that it is safe. With respect to the UL mark, respondents indicated that the UL mark is understood to mean that the product is safe and meets high quality standards. Responding bicycle helmet manufacturers identified the CE, SEI and TÜV marks. The responses indicated that manufacturers believe that consumers understand the CE and TÜV certification marks to mean that the product conforms to government safety standards. Closely related to that belief is that consumers understand the certification mark to mean that the product meets high quality standards and is safe. With respect to the SEI, it is believed that consumers understand it to mean that the product meets high quality standards, it is permitted to be sold and it is safe. One response indicated that under Chinese law, ISO 9000 certification is required for toy manufacturers who export out of China. Other sources agree with this, but maintain that the certification requirements are seldom applied. However, one microwave oven respondent added that while there are not any concrete requirements yet for ISO 9000 certification by government agencies in the category of home electrical appliances, some distributors are demanding such certification for certain products.

42 Responses from toy manufacturers indicated that in the European Union testing the product takes between three weeks and two months. The cost of testing and certification ranges from US$ 300 to US$ 2 000 per product. American toy manufacturers indicated that the cost of testing their products ranges between US$ 500 and US$ 800 per product and that it takes at least one week to conduct the tests. According to one response from a toy manufacturer, obtaining the ST mark in Japan takes approximately one week. The applicant submits two samples for inspection at a cost of between US$ 40 and US$ 160. Then the product is subjected to the sanitation test which costs between US$ 200 and US$ 500. In both the European Union and the United States, lawn mower manufacturers indicated that the time involved in the entire process is estimated to take between two and six months. The actual physical testing of the product in both markets takes approximately one week. The cost estimates ranged from about US$ 20 000 in the United States to US$ 30 000 in Europe. In the United States, third-party testing and certification by a non-government body involves the following steps for lawn mowers: agreement between the manufacturer and the association; agreement between the manufacturer and the certifier; arrangements for on-site visit by certifier; actual certification; possible follow-up; final report; and application of certification mark to product. This process takes between one and two months depending on the size of the manufacturer, and the number of products and models to be certified. The lawn mower manufacturer is then monitored two times each year. In Europe, the product is presented to the testing body. Testing for conformance to the Noise Emissions Directive generally takes one day and testing to the Machine Directive takes two days. After testing is completed, the report is then filed. The process for testing and certifying microwave ovens in the United States involving third-party testing by UL costs approximately US$ 20 000 per model according to respondents. The process takes between four and five months for new models and involves the application, submission and testing of the product, approval and factory audits. In Japan, the process takes approximately three months and costs about US$ 10 000. In Europe, the process takes approximately three months and costs between US$ 10 000 and US$ 15 000. According to the responses from bicycle helmet manufacturers, the process in Europe takes approximately three months from beginning to end. The costs for testing and certification were estimated at US$ 2 000 per model. In the United States, testing and certification was estimated to take between two and six weeks and costs about US$ 1 000. The SEI

certification process was described as involving the following: application (one week); shipment of the sample product to the designated laboratory (one day); testing (one week); and authorisation to produce certified product (one day). In addition, a factory audit and "QA" system approval is needed which takes at least one month.

[43] In Australia, under the auspices of the Australian trade practices act (1974) a mandatory consumer product safety standard has been prescribed for toys for children under three years of age. The mandatory standard calls into law aspects of the otherwise voluntary Australian standard AS1647.2-1991 (Constructional requirements). The European standard for toys is made up of five parts, four of which have been already published. These are EN71-1 (mechanical and physical properties); EN71-2 (flammability); EN71-3 (migration of certain elements); and EN71-5 (chemical toys other than experimental sets). Reference was also made to HD271 S1 EN50088 (electrical toys). Respondents in the United States referred to the voluntary ASTM standard F963-95 (consumer safety specification on toy safety) which was considered to be a performance standard.

[44] For microwave ovens the international standard has also been adopted as a European standard EN60335-2-25 and transposed by all the national standards organisations in CENELEC. In Canada there are a number of standards applicable to microwave ovens, including CAN/CSA C22.2 No.150-M89 (Microwave ovens which deals with electrical safety aspects), CAN/CSA E335-2-25-94 (Safety of Household and Similar Electrical Appliances -- Part 2: Particular Requirements for Microwave Ovens). This is the adopted IEC international standard with modifications. Respondents also cited CAN/CSA C388-M89 - (Energy Consumption Test Methods for Household Microwave Ovens) which is an energy performance standard which respondents felt could have an impact on food safety. The official Mexican safety standard applicable to microwave ovens is NOM-001-SCFI-1993 "Requerimentos de seguridad y métodos de prueba para la aprobación de tipo de aparatos electrónicos de uso doméstico alimentado por diferentes fuentes de energía eléctrica" -- "Safety requirements and testing methods for type approval of household electronic apparatus by different sources of electrical power."

[45] The Australian standard that was quoted is AS2063 (lightweight protective helmets for use in pedal cycling horse-riding and other applications requiring similar protection) and AS2063.2-1990 (helmets for pedal cyclists). The Canadian standard is CAN/CSA D113.2-M89 (Cycling Helmets). For bicycle helmets there is the European draft standard prEN1078 helmets for pedal cyclists/skateboard/roller skates. In Japan there is an approval standard for bicycle helmets, CPSA 0056, which was established in March 1983 by the Japanese consumer product safety association. The standard describes appearance, structure, material, strength and shock absorption of helmets. Products which meet the standards are allowed to bear the "SG mark". The SG mark system is a voluntary certification scheme. In the United States there is an ANSI standard and a standard developed by a private institute, the SNELL foundation.

[46] In Canada the standard is CAN/CSA C22.2 No.147 - Motor Operated Gardening Appliances. The European draft standard prEN836 on garden equipment which refers to powered lawn mowers will after ratification be transposed by all the European standards organisations. This standard uses as a base the ISO standard 5395. The Mexican safety standard applicable to electric lawn mowers is NMX-J-508-1194-ANCE referring to electrical appliances' safety

requirements specifications and testing methods. In the United States there is a mandatory standard from the Consumer Product Safety Commission relating to walk-behind mowers, CPSC 1205. There are also two relevant voluntary standards from ANSI, ANSI B71.1 and B71.4.

47   In Australia reference was made to European and US standards in drafting the Australian national standard. For the Australian bike helmets standard existing US industry standards (developed by SNELL foundation) were consulted in the development of the current edition, but the Committee felt that they were not appropriate or adequate in several areas. The Canadian standard CAN/CSA EE5-25-94 is an adopted IEC standard which was reviewed by a consensus-based Committee and revised so that the adapted standard offered the same degree of safety as the Canadian standard. The use of international standards as a basis is part of Canadian harmonisation policy. For lawnmowers the draft European standard prEN836 uses as a base the international standard ISO-5395. In Europe the international standard for microwave ovens has been adopted as the European Standard by CENELEC and transposed by the national standards bodies. In Japan the bicycle helmet standard (CPSA 0056) was influenced by the Japanese industrial standard (JIS T 8134) (protective helmets for bicycle users). In Mexico ovens are subject to the Tec-65-1985 standard safety requirements regarding household electronic apparatus. The Mexican lawn mower standard was developed after examining both the relevant US standards and international standards. The existing UK standard for headforms and the draft European standard for bike helmets have been consulted in the course of the current revision due for publication in 1996. The US standards themselves were drafted with extensive reference to the provisions contained in existing standards once a proposed outline of the standard had been first developed. Requirements from the existing related standards were then inserted into this outline. It was felt that this approach helped to develop consistent terminology as well as taking advantage of existing concepts.

48   In the electro-technical sector in Europe it is the policy of the European standards body CENELEC to adopt where possible international standards. At the national level in Europe member states national standards bodies are required to implement the results of European standardisation work and remove any conflicting standards from their catalogues.

49   Respondents stated that generally that all interested parties were welcome to participate in the development of standards and specifically cited manufacturers, consumer organisations and test labs. Sometimes there is a framework for such participation, as is the case in Mexico. The right to representation in the standards process is assured in art. 47 of the Mexican federal law on Metrology and Standardisation which requires each draft proposal of a particular mandatory standard to be published in the Diario official (DOF Official Register). Once the draft proposal has been published, a period of 90 days is allowed for receiving comments and suggestions from the general public, including any foreign entity that may be interested in the standard. Then the committee formulates the final version of the standard, taking into consideration the observations received. In Australia all the work is jointly done with standards New Zealand and other national standards bodies may nominate non-voting members who participate in committee work by correspondence. Drafts for public comment are regularly sent to Malaysia, the United Kingdom and other overseas standards bodies with a significant interest. In Canada, SA's Technical Committees are required to have a balanced matrix of voting members. Representatives from industry, regulatory authorities, consumers,

trade associations, safety officials, and retailers are encouraged to serve as voting members on the Committee. In Europe considerable efforts have been made to open up the standardisation process since the adoption of the New Approach, and this is reflected in the rules and regulations of the standards bodies.

50. In the areas of bicycle helmets, in Australia the National Injury Surveillance Unit (NISU) statistics indicate that from 1970 to 1990 the rate of bicycle fatalities per 1000 people has fallen by around 20 per cent. This has primarily been attributed to compulsory use of helmets complying with AS 2063.2. While Canadian injury records are not extensive and only come from a sample of hospitals, the data indicates an increase in the wearing of helmets and a decrease in serious head injuries since the introduction of the CSA helmet certification programme. The introduction of a lawnmower standard in Mexico has reduced the risk of injury in areas such as electrical shocks caused by electrical discharges or leakage, accidentally or provoked burns when overheated accessible parts are touched, injuries and material damages from mechanical instabilities and or construction deficiencies. In Canada the microwave standard had brought about a reduction of the fire risk then associated with these products. Canadian injury data on microwaves report fewer injuries now associated with these products. However, consumer representatives in recent years have expressed concern about food safety related to increased performance (e.g. unevenness of heating, temperature outputs, etc.). In the United States information on injury data is circulated by the Federal Consumer Product Safety Commission. In relation to lawnmowers, since the advent of CPSC 1205 in 1982 there has been a reduction of about 35 per cent in hand injuries from rotary walk behind mowers.

51. The 1996 edition of the Australian helmets standard will address increasing the range of sizes subjected to physical testing, improving the specification of the localised load distribution test to reduce inter-laboratory variability, expanding user information and labelling, and reducing recommended helmet mass. These standards need to be reviewed regularly in light of current research. In Canada, there is little support for standards activity in this product area due to the lack of domestic manufacturers located. More research needs to be done on safety and health issues to determine if changes are required. In the United states one respondent expressed the opinion that the following considerations will need to be taken into account in any future revision of the lawnmower standard: mowers have 5.5 year evolution period, 20 per cent of all accidents occur within first eight hours of use, 20 per cent of all accident victims are immigrants, usually Spanish-speaking with little mechanical background, and future standards improvements based on new technology will be hard to measure in improved safety due to the already low accident rate.

52. In relation to the IEC, one respondent cited the need for a greater commitment from the US and Asian national committees to implement the results of IEC work. Another respondent identified the need to remove special national conditions in IEC standards which allowed national deviations from the standards. Other respondents called for harmonisation between EN standard and UL/ANSI standards, and for co-operation between governments and standards associations to develop and harmonise compatible standards.

53. The cost of initial accreditation of testing facilities ranged from US$ 215 to 20 000 while initial accreditation for certification programmes/facilities ranged from $86 to $15 000. The

cost of annual maintenance of each testing facilities accreditation ranged from $1 000 to $8 000 and that of certification facility accreditation around $1 000.

[54] With respect to bicycle helmets the harmonisation of testing procedures, in this instance for all types of helmets, was proposed as one means to improve their cost-effectiveness or reliability. In relation to microwaves it was proposed that certification must be subjected to a cost-benefit analysis in order to assure a benefit for the consumer. One respondent advocated shortening the period permitted for a manufacturer to continue production to an obsolete standard. In Europe CENELEC Memorandum No. 6 deals with this issue and is currently being amended.

[55] Specific examples that were given included the use of standards, the mutual recognition of test results and certification in the EU, and recognised accreditation under the EAC-MLA.

[56] These notes are written by the author in a personal capacity and do not necessarily reflect those of the WTO, its members or its Secretariat.

[57] The market barriers listed in the poll, and their resulting ranking, from the most to the least important were: (1) administrative barriers, (2) national standards and regulations, (3) physical frontier delays, (4) community law, (5) restrictions in the capital market, (6/7) differences in VAT/regulations of freight transport, and (8) government procurement. Source: Table 1.1, Checchini (1988), "The European Challenge, 1992, The Benefits of a Single Market."

[58] Financial Times (September 4, 1986), "Japanese Ski Makers Freeze out the Opposition."

[59] The data has been compiled by the WTO, based on submitted notifications under the Standards Codes between 1980 and 1994. The grouping into various categories is sometimes dubious as countries may have given several objectives for their national standards and regulations. In those cases, notifications have been classified under more than one category. The classification is preliminary and subject to revision.

[60] "A Member preparing, adopting or applying a technical regulation which may have a significant effect on trade of other Members, shall, upon the request of another Member, explain the justification for that technical regulation in terms of provisions of paragraphs 2 to 4" (Article 2.5). Paragraph 2, in turn, states that "Members shall ensure that in respect of technical regulations are not prepared, adopted or applied with a view to or with the effect of creating unnecessary obstacles to international trade. For this purpose, technical regulations shall not be more trade-restrictive than necessary to fulfil a legitimate objective, taking account the risks non-fulfilment would create" (Article 2.2). Paragraph 3 goes on by requiring that "technical regulations shall not be maintained if the circumstances or objectives giving rise to their adoption no longer exist or if the changed circumstances or objectives can be addressed in a less trade-restrictive manner" (Article 2.3).

MAIN SALES OUTLETS OF OECD PUBLICATIONS
PRINCIPAUX POINTS DE VENTE DES PUBLICATIONS DE L'OCDE

AUSTRALIA – AUSTRALIE
D.A. Information Services
648 Whitehorse Road, P.O.B 163
Mitcham, Victoria 3132   Tel. (03) 9210.7777
                             Fax: (03) 9210.7788

AUSTRIA – AUTRICHE
Gerold & Co.
Graben 31
Wien I   Tel. (0222) 533.50.14
                             Fax: (0222) 512.47.31.29

BELGIUM – BELGIQUE
Jean De Lannoy
Avenue du Roi, Koningslaan 202
B-1060 Bruxelles   Tel. (02) 538.51.69/538.08.41
                             Fax: (02) 538.08.41

CANADA
Renouf Publishing Company Ltd.
1294 Algoma Road
Ottawa, ON K1B 3W8   Tel. (613) 741.4333
                             Fax: (613) 741.5439
Stores:
61 Sparks Street
Ottawa, ON K1P 5R1   Tel. (613) 238.8985
12 Adelaide Street West
Toronto, ON M5H 1L6   Tel. (416) 363.3171
                             Fax: (416)363.59.63

Les Éditions La Liberté Inc.
3020 Chemin Sainte-Foy
Sainte-Foy, PQ G1X 3V6   Tel. (418) 658.3763
                             Fax: (418) 658.3763

Federal Publications Inc.
165 University Avenue, Suite 701
Toronto, ON M5H 3B8   Tel. (416) 860.1611
                             Fax: (416) 860.1608

Les Publications Fédérales
1185 Université
Montréal, QC H3B 3A7   Tel. (514) 954.1633
                             Fax: (514) 954.1635

CHINA – CHINE
China National Publications Import
Export Corporation (CNPIEC)
16 Gongti E. Road, Chaoyang District
P.O. Box 88 or 50
Beijing 100704 PR   Tel. (01) 506.6688
                             Fax: (01) 506.3101

CHINESE TAIPEI – TAIPEI CHINOIS
Good Faith Worldwide Int'l. Co. Ltd.
9th Floor, No. 118, Sec. 2
Chung Hsiao E. Road
Taipei   Tel. (02) 391.7396/391.7397
                             Fax: (02) 394.9176

DENMARK – DANEMARK
Munksgaard Book and Subscription Service
35, Nørre Søgade, P.O. Box 2148
DK-1016 København K   Tel. (33) 12.85.70
                             Fax: (33) 12.93.87

J. H. Schultz Information A/S,
Herstedvang 12,
DK – 2620 Albertslung   Tel. 43 63 23 00
                             Fax: 43 63 19 69
Internet: s-info@inet.uni-c.dk

EGYPT – ÉGYPTE
Middle East Observer
41 Sherif Street
Cairo   Tel. 392.6919
                             Fax: 360-6804

FINLAND – FINLANDE
Akateeminen Kirjakauppa
Keskuskatu 1, P.O. Box 128
00100 Helsinki
Subscription Services/Agence d'abonnements :
P.O. Box 23
00371 Helsinki   Tel. (358 0) 121 4416
                       Fax: (358 0) 121.4450

FRANCE
OECD/OCDE
Mail Orders/Commandes par correspondance :
2, rue André-Pascal
75775 Paris Cedex 16   Tel. (33-1) 45.24.82.00
                       Fax: (33-1) 49.10.42.76
                       Telex: 640048 OCDE
Internet: Compte.PUBSINQ@oecd.org

Orders via Minitel, France only/
Commandes par Minitel, France exclusivement :
36 15 OCDE

OECD Bookshop/Librairie de l'OCDE :
33, rue Octave-Feuillet
75016 Paris   Tél. (33-1) 45.24.81.81
                            (33-1) 45.24.81.67

Dawson
B.P. 40
91121 Palaiseau Cedex   Tel. 69.10.47.00
                            Fax: 64.54.83.26

Documentation Française
29, quai Voltaire
75007 Paris   Tel. 40.15.70.00

Economica
49, rue Héricart
75015 Paris   Tel. 45.75.05.67
                            Fax: 40.58.15.70

Gibert Jeune (Droit-Économie)
6, place Saint-Michel
75006 Paris   Tel. 43.25.91.19

Librairie du Commerce International
10, avenue d'Iéna
75016 Paris   Tel. 40.73.34.60

Librairie Dunod
Université Paris-Dauphine
Place du Maréchal-de-Lattre-de-Tassigny
75016 Paris   Tel. 44.05.40.13

Librairie Lavoisier
11, rue Lavoisier
75008 Paris   Tel. 42.65.39.95

Librairie des Sciences Politiques
30, rue Saint-Guillaume
75007 Paris   Tel. 45.48.36.02

P.U.F.
49, boulevard Saint-Michel
75005 Paris   Tel. 43.25.83.40

Librairie de l'Université
12a, rue Nazareth
13100 Aix-en-Provence   Tel. (16) 42.26.18.08

Documentation Française
165, rue Garibaldi
69003 Lyon   Tel. (16) 78.63.32.23

Librairie Decitre
29, place Bellecour
69002 Lyon   Tel. (16) 72.40.54.54

Librairie Sauramps
Le Triangle
34967 Montpellier Cedex 2   Tel. (16) 67.58.85.15
                            Fax: (16) 67.58.27.36

A la Sorbonne Actual
23, rue de l'Hôtel-des-Postes
06000 Nice   Tel. (16) 93.13.77.75
                            Fax: (16) 93.80.75.69

GERMANY – ALLEMAGNE
OECD Bonn Centre
August-Bebel-Allee 6
D-53175 Bonn   Tel. (0228) 959.120
                       Fax: (0228) 959.12.17

GREECE – GRÈCE
Librairie Kauffmann
Stadiou 28
10564 Athens   Tel. (01) 32.55.321
                       Fax: (01) 32.30.320

HONG-KONG
Swindon Book Co. Ltd.
Astoria Bldg. 3F
34 Ashley Road, Tsimshatsui
Kowloon, Hong Kong   Tel. 2376.2062
                       Fax: 2376.0685

HUNGARY – HONGRIE
Euro Info Service
Margitsziget, Európa Ház
1138 Budapest   Tel. (1) 111.62.16
                       Fax: (1) 111.60.61

ICELAND – ISLANDE
Mál Mog Menning
Laugavegi 18, Pósthólf 392
121 Reykjavik   Tel. (1) 552.4240
                       Fax: (1) 562.3523

INDIA – INDE
Oxford Book and Stationery Co.
Scindia House
New Delhi 110001   Tel. (11) 331.5896/5308
                       Fax: (11) 332.5993
17 Park Street
Calcutta 700016   Tel. 240832

INDONESIA – INDONÉSIE
Pdii-Lipi
P.O. Box 4298
Jakarta 12042   Tel. (21) 573.34.67
                       Fax: (21) 573.34.67

IRELAND – IRLANDE
Government Supplies Agency
Publications Section
4/5 Harcourt Road
Dublin 2   Tel. 661.31.11
                       Fax: 475.27.60

ISRAEL – ISRAËL
Praedicta
5 Shatner Street
P.O. Box 34030
Jerusalem 91430   Tel. (2) 52.84.90/1/2
                       Fax: (2) 52.84.93

R.O.Y. International
P.O. Box 13056
Tel Aviv 61130   Tel. (3) 546 1423
                       Fax: (3) 546 1442

Palestinian Authority/Middle East:
INDEX Information Services
P.O.B. 19502
Jerusalem   Tel. (2) 27.12.19
                       Fax: (2) 27.16.34

ITALY – ITALIE
Libreria Commissionaria Sansoni
Via Duca di Calabria 1/1
50125 Firenze   Tel. (055) 64.54.15
                       Fax: (055) 64.12.57
Via Bartolini 29
20155 Milano   Tel. (02) 36.50.83

Editrice e Libreria Herder
Piazza Montecitorio 120
00186 Roma   Tel. 679.46.28
                       Fax: 678.47.51

Libreria Hoepli
Via Hoepli 5
20121 Milano   Tel. (02) 86.54.46
                        Fax: (02) 805.28.86

Libreria Scientifica
Dott. Lucio de Biasio 'Aeiou'
Via Coronelli, 6
20146 Milano   Tel. (02) 48.95.45.52
                        Fax: (02) 48.95.45.48

JAPAN – JAPON
OECD Tokyo Centre
Landic Akasaka Building
2-3-4 Akasaka, Minato-ku
Tokyo 107   Tel. (81.3) 3586.2016
                        Fax: (81.3) 3584.7929

KOREA – CORÉE
Kyobo Book Centre Co. Ltd.
P.O. Box 1658, Kwang Hwa Moon
Seoul   Tel. 730.78.91
                        Fax: 735.00.30

MALAYSIA – MALAISIE
University of Malaya Bookshop
University of Malaya
P.O. Box 1127, Jalan Pantai Baru
59700 Kuala Lumpur
Malaysia   Tel. 756.5000/756.5425
                        Fax: 756.3246

MEXICO – MEXIQUE
OECD Mexico Centre
Edificio INFOTEC
Av. San Fernando no. 37
Col. Toriello Guerra
Tlalpan C.P. 14050
Mexico D.F.   Tel. (525) 665 47 99
                        Fax: (525) 606 13 07

Revistas y Periodicos Internacionales S.A. de C.V.
Florencia 57 - 1004
Mexico, D.F. 06600   Tel. 207.81.00
                        Fax: 208.39.79

NETHERLANDS – PAYS-BAS
SDU Uitgeverij Plantijnstraat
Externe Fondsen
Postbus 20014
2500 EA's-Gravenhage   Tel. (070) 37.89.880
Voor bestellingen: Fax: (070) 34.75.778

**NEW ZEALAND –
NOUVELLE-ZÉLANDE**
GPLegislation Services
P.O. Box 12418
Thorndon, Wellington   Tel. (04) 496.5655
                        Fax: (04) 496.5698

NORWAY – NORVÈGE
NIC INFO A/S
Bertrand Narvesens vei 2
P.O. Box 6512 Etterstad
0606 Oslo 6   Tel. (022) 57.33.00
                        Fax: (022) 68.19.01

PAKISTAN
Mirza Book Agency
65 Shahrah Quaid-E-Azam
Lahore 54000   Tel. (42) 735.36.01
                        Fax: (42) 576.37.14

PHILIPPINE – PHILIPPINES
International Booksource Center Inc.
Rm 179/920 Cityland 10 Condo Tower 2
HV dela Costa Ext cor Valero St.
Makati Metro Manila   Tel. (632) 817 9676
                        Fax: (632) 817 1741

POLAND – POLOGNE
Ars Polona
00-950 Warszawa
Krakowskie Przedmieácie 7   Tel. (22) 264760
                            Fax: (22) 268673

PORTUGAL
Livraria Portugal
Rua do Carmo 70-74
Apart. 2681
1200 Lisboa   Tel. (01) 347.49.82/5
                        Fax: (01) 347.02.64

SINGAPORE – SINGAPOUR
Gower Asia Pacific Pte Ltd.
Golden Wheel Building
41, Kallang Pudding Road, No. 04-03
Singapore 1334   Tel. 741.5166
                        Fax: 742.9356

SPAIN – ESPAGNE
Mundi-Prensa Libros S.A.
Castelló 37, Apartado 1223
Madrid 28001   Tel. (91) 431.33.99
                        Fax: (91) 575.39.98

Mundi-Prensa Barcelona
Consell de Cent No. 391
08009 – Barcelona   Tel. (93) 488.34.92
                        Fax: (93) 487.76.59

Llibreria de la Generalitat
Palau Moja
Rambla dels Estudis, 118
08002 – Barcelona
        (Subscripcions) Tel. (93) 318.80.12
        (Publicacions) Tel. (93) 302.67.23
                        Fax: (93) 412.18.54

SRI LANKA
Centre for Policy Research
c/o Colombo Agencies Ltd.
No. 300-304, Galle Road
Colombo 3   Tel. (1) 574240, 573551-2
                    Fax: (1) 575394, 510711

SWEDEN – SUÈDE
CE Fritzes AB
S–106 47 Stockholm   Tel. (08) 690.90.90
                        Fax: (08) 20.50.21

Subscription Agency/Agence d'abonnements :
Wennergren-Williams Info AB
P.O. Box 1305
171 25 Solna   Tel. (08) 705.97.50
                        Fax: (08) 27.00.71

SWITZERLAND – SUISSE
Maditec S.A. (Books and Periodicals - Livres
et périodiques)
Chemin des Palettes 4
Case postale 266
1020 Renens VD 1   Tel. (021) 635.08.65
                        Fax: (021) 635.07.80

Librairie Payot S.A.
4, place Pépinet
CP 3212
1002 Lausanne   Tel. (021) 320.25.11
                        Fax: (021) 320.25.14

Librairie Unilivres
6, rue de Candolle
1205 Genève   Tel. (022) 320.26.23
                        Fax: (022) 329.73.18

Subscription Agency/Agence d'abonnements :
Dynapresse Marketing S.A.
38, avenue Vibert
1227 Carouge   Tel. (022) 308.07.89
                        Fax: (022) 308.07.99

See also – Voir aussi :
OECD Bonn Centre
August-Bebel-Allee 6
D-53175 Bonn (Germany)   Tel. (0228) 959.120
                           Fax: (0228) 959.12.17

THAILAND – THAÏLANDE
Suksit Siam Co. Ltd.
113, 115 Fuang Nakhon Rd.
Opp. Wat Rajbopith
Bangkok 10200   Tel. (662) 225.9531/2
                        Fax: (662) 222.5188

TRINIDAD & TOBAGO
SSL Systematics Studies Limited
9 Watts Street
Curepe
Trinadad & Tobago, W.I.   Tel. (1809) 645.3475
                           Fax: (1809) 662.5654

TUNISIA – TUNISIE
Grande Librairie Spécialisée
Fendri Ali
Avenue Haffouz Imm El-Intilaka
Bloc B 1 Sfax 3000   Tel. (216-4) 296 855
                        Fax: (216-4) 298.270

TURKEY – TURQUIE
Kültür Yayinlari Is-Türk Ltd. Sti.
Atatürk Bulvari No. 191/Kat 13
Kavaklidere/Ankara
                Tel. (312) 428.11.40 Ext. 2458
                        Fax: (312) 417 24 90
Dolmabahce Cad. No. 29
Besiktas/Istanbul   Tel. (212) 260 7188

UNITED KINGDOM – ROYAUME-UNI
HMSO
Gen. enquiries   Tel. (0171) 873 0011
Postal orders only:
P.O. Box 276, London SW8 5DT
Personal Callers HMSO Bookshop
49 High Holborn, London WC1V 6HB
                        Fax: (0171) 873 8463
Branches at: Belfast, Birmingham, Bristol,
Edinburgh, Manchester

UNITED STATES – ÉTATS-UNIS
OECD Washington Center
2001 L Street N.W., Suite 650
Washington, D.C. 20036-4922 Tel. (202) 785.6323
                        Fax: (202) 785.0350
Internet: washcont@oecd.org

Subscriptions to OECD periodicals may also be
placed through main subscription agencies.

Les abonnements aux publications périodiques de
l'OCDE peuvent être souscrits auprès des
principales agences d'abonnement.

Orders and inquiries from countries where Distribu-
tors have not yet been appointed should be sent to:
OECD Publications, 2, rue André-Pascal, 75775
Paris Cedex 16, France.

Les commandes provenant de pays où l'OCDE n'a
pas encore désigné de distributeur peuvent être
adressées aux Éditions de l'OCDE, 2, rue André-
Pascal, 75775 Paris Cedex 16, France.

                                        5-1996

OECD PUBLICATIONS, 2, rue André-Pascal, 75775 PARIS CEDEX 16
PRINTED IN FRANCE
(24 96 01 1) ISBN 92-64-15298-9 – No. 49033 1996